RESURRECTION FIRE

WHERE DEAD THINGS COME ALIVE

RESURRECTION FIRE

WHERE DEAD THINGS COME ALIVE

DAWN CHRISTENSEN

Hunter Entertainment Network
Colorado Springs, Colorado

Resurrection Fire: Where Dead Things Come Alive
Copyright © 2021 by Dawn Christensen
First Edition: January 2022

All rights reserved. No part of this book may be reproduced or transmitted in any form or by any means without written permission of the publisher, except in brief quotes or reviews. Unless otherwise noted, all Scripture is taken from the New King James Version® (NKJV). Copyright © 1982 by Thomas Nelson. Used by permission. All rights reserved.

All memories and recollections are that of the author and her experiences throughout her life. Publisher holds no responsibility for the personal content shared within this book.

To order products, or for any other correspondence:

Hunter Entertainment Network
Colorado Springs, Colorado 80840
www.hunter-ent-net.com
Tel. (253) 906-2160
E-mail: contact@hunter-entertainment.com
Or reach us on Instagram at: Hunter Entertainment Network
"Offering God's Heart to a Dying World"

This book and all other Hunter Entertainment Network™ Hunter Heart Publishing™, and Hunter Heart Kids™ books are available at Christian bookstores and distributors worldwide.

Chief Editor: Deborah G. Hunter
Book cover design: Phil Coles Independent Design
Layout & logos: Exousia Marketing Group www.exousiamg.com
ISBN: 9798791038562
Printed in the United States of America.

Dedication

I dedicate this to my first love, Jesus, and precious Holy Spirit, the Lover of my soul, I give You all the Glory and Honor because I'm nothing without You. You're my perfect surprise gift of comfort, strength, and never-failing love. King Jesus, Your presence is superior and my protected hiding place. I drench every reader's heart and mind in Your blood Jesus, which is the most powerful substance in the universe. It is stronger than any anti-depressant, anti-anxiety, anti-viral, and opioid medications.

To all the abused, afflicted, addicted, and mentally ill. You are who your Heavenly Father says you are.

Holy Spirit speak through me to release your Love, Glory, Presence, and Holy Fire to break the power of all darkness and bondage of abuse, affliction, addiction, suicide, and "mental illness." Thank You for setting me free from a tormented mind, relentless physical and psychological pain of abuse, trauma, fear, rejection, and abandonment. Father God, I thank You that You're not a respecter of persons and every person who reads this will encounter Your love and freedom.

Acknowledgments

I want to thank my children Nathaniel, Heaven, Amya, and Nevaeh. I love each of you and you individually bring uniqueness, powerful strength, and great influence to your generation. Being your mother is an honor and my greatest gift, I'm so blessed God trusts me with your hearts.

My mother Delores Gooden, you taught me how to love everyone, see no color, and quickly forgive those who hurt us. Rest in Heaven's Glory.

My parents Robert and Rose Dame, your love and marriage for nearly 40 years lets me know it's still possible. Dad, it richly blesses me to see your faith and boldness for God grow deeper.

I want to acknowledge some particularly important people that have helped me walk through my healing and deliverance. Thank you for believing in me!

Marc and Lydia Buchheit: Healing The Northwest Ministries
Chris Overstreet: Compassion to Action
Dustin and Robynn Langley: Peninsula Life Church
Tom and Katy Cornell, Jared Schmitz: Sozo Church

Bill Dickerson: Gateway Ministries
Benjamin Tucker
Carol BoRich
Carroll Kees
Judy Peterson
Cedric and Angie Van Duyns
Julie Bennett
Sharon Rueckert
Lori Jean Medina: Lion's Light International
Deborah G. Hunter: Hunter Entertainment Network
Dr. Richard Leone
Kirsty Docken, EAMP, LAc

Foreword

A life that has been changed and transformed by the power and saving grace of Jesus is the greatest miracle. Throughout the Bible, we see God at work. We see Jesus calling many from all types of backgrounds to follow Him. Jesus has compassion for the multitudes but also for the *one*.

Jesus saw Zacchaeus while he was in the tree, and He called him by name. Jesus walked by the sea and saw fishermen, and He called them, as well, to follow Him. I am inspired by the life of Jesus, and He chooses people to invite to follow Him.

Jesus disturbed the religious circle. He told those that thought they were right with God that He came for the sick. This was a slap in the face of many because that meant He placed a value on them and what He valued really showed up in whom He picked and how He spent His time.

Do you need a fresh start? Do you need forgiveness?

When Jesus called Matthew the tax collector, Matthew did not fit in with some of the crowds but somehow that did not bother Jesus. Matthew belonged to Jesus. When Jesus sat at the table with Matthew, the former tax collector, His disciples, and other sinners, Jesus, I am sure, felt so comfortable with them. I can only imagine how Matthew was feeling. Matthew was just recently chosen and now he was amongst many others that were selected before him, but there was a group of people somehow that saw what was going on. They questioned Jesus and His discernment on why He would ever eat with these types of people. Jesus, knowing what was going on, decided to remind them that this was the reason He came and for those He came for.

Are you in need of a Savior? His name is Jesus, and He has the power to save, heal, and deliver.

I am proud of Dawn for writing *Resurrection Fire*. I love her offering that she has given to the Lord. Her offering is her life, and this book is a token of it to help but reach one more soul for Jesus.

"For I am not ashamed of the gospel of Christ, for it is the power of God to salvation for everyone who believes, for the Jew first and also for the Greek. For in it the righteousness of God is revealed from faith to faith; as it is written, "The just shall live by faith." Romans 1: 16-17

There is a generation on the rise that is bold and honest to declare, "I was lost and broken, but Jesus found me and put me on the narrow road that leads to life."

Jesus is the only way, and His grace empowers us to keep saying "Yes" to Him with our love because He first loved us.

Dawn, keep writing. I am proud of you.

Chris Overstreet
Compassiontoaction.com

Table of Contents

Introduction 1

Chapter 1: Where it All Began 5

Chapter 2: Sexual Abuse: The Stealing of My Innocence 13

Chapter 3: New Beginnings… or at Least I Thought?............ 21

Chapter 4: Forced to Grow Up too Soon 29

Chapter 5: Patterns of Emotional, Mental & Sexual Abuse..... 39

Chapter 6: Generational Curses 53

Chapter 7: Processing Through Your Pain.............................. 63

Chapter 8: The Importance of Counseling & Therapy 83

Chapter 9: Inner Healing & Deliverance 95

Chapter 10: Lazarus… Come Forth!...................................... 109

Conclusion 117

Resources 119

Prayers 123

Meet the Author 125

Bibliography 127

Introduction

*"These things He said, and after that He said to them, "Our friend Lazarus sleeps, but I go that I may **wake him up**."*

John 11:11 (emphasis)

The narrative of Lazarus in the Bible is a story of patience, process, perseverance, purpose, and ultimately, the promise of God to resurrect the "dead things" in our lives. When Lazarus passed, Mary and Martha sent for Jesus to come, as they were fully expecting He would heal and raise him from the dead. They had witnessed countless healings and miracles performed by Jesus, so why would this be any different. Lazarus was loved deeply by Him, and both sisters knew this intimately. Why did Jesus take so long to come? It had been four days, and by this time, the body was emitting a foul odor and there seemed to be no hope left to save Lazarus. Jesus came on the fourth day. Jewish mysticism teaches that a deceased person's spirit remains around the body for up to three days after death before departing. It was well-known in Israel 2,000 years ago that someone deceased could come back to life during this 3-day period but not afterwards.[i]

On the fourth day, the spirit left the body and went to Sheol, or Hades, and there was no hope for life without a miracle. Also, by the fourth day in Israel's hot climate, advanced decay would be destroying the body and the stench would have been overwhelming. When Jesus called Lazarus to life from the dead and healed his rotted corpse, the people knew that He was the true Messiah, performing genuine miracles as the prophets had foretold!

Mary, Martha, and the many surrounding his tomb were distraught, dismayed, and discouraged. They had lost hope that their brother would be raised from the dead, because it was unheard of for such a resurrection to take place after three days. Jesus' lesson for them all proved to be one of the greatest miracles recorded in the Bible. The story of Lazarus is filled with life lessons, principles, and ultimately, faith. Our lives are filled with ups and downs, and twists and turns. We know the Word of God and celebrate the stories we read within the holy scriptures, but when we come face to face with our own issues: sickness, disease, death, loss of marriage, prodigal children, loss of jobs, homes, and everything you could possibly think of, we seem to lose hope that God will *resurrect* the "dead things" in our own lives. We can believe for others, and pray them through to their healing, deliverance, and salvation, but when it comes to us, we hit that brick wall and fall into that bottomless pit of despair and destruction.

Resurrection Fire

God, through the story of Lazarus, compels and commands us to "wake up!" We are encouraged, exhorted, and empowered to trust the Father, no matter how devastating the situation may look, or even seem, to our natural senses. Each of us must endure the process of preparation in our lives. So often, we want God to simply "snap His fingers" and get us out of those "dead places," instead of walking along our journey with Him through the process, building our trust and faith in Him toward the promise of His fulfillment in our lives. Listen, I fully understand. My life has been riddled with hurt, pain, disappointment, and destruction, and more things than even I may be willing to admit. From as early as I can remember, my life began with scores of abuse. In the beginning, I simply thought this was "normal." I can almost say I *died* before I even began to live. Much of my life has been stolen from me, but God, in His infinite love and purpose for my existence, has *raised me from the dead* and placed me on the path toward my destiny in Christ!

I have learned so much along my journey, and everything that the enemy meant for harm, Father God has turned around for my good. I may not be fully where I want to be, but I am confident and sure I am *exactly* where He needs me to be in this season of my life. I am a work in progress, and each victory brings glory to His name. Whatever your life story has produced, trust and believe that He will use it for great purpose. He uses it all; He leaves nothing untouched! The things that look dead, with no possible hope of being restored. The *God of the Impossi-*

ble is working on your behalf and mine, along with our families and relationships, including our marriages.

I pray and declare as you read this book, there will be New Beginnings and New Life, Hope Restored, Reset, and Reboot... *Resurrection Fire* released into your life for a testimony and a witness of the love and goodness of our Lord and Savior, Jesus Christ. Get ready for the dead things in your life to COME ALIVE!

Chapter 1

Where it All Began

*"For You formed my inward parts;
You covered me in my mother's womb.
I will praise You, for I am fearfully and wonderfully made;
Marvelous are Your works,
And that my soul knows very well.
My frame was not hidden from You,
When I was made in secret,
And skillfully wrought in the lowest parts of the earth."*

~Psalm 139: 13-16~

I was born on September 26, 1978, in St. Louis, Missouri. My parents were married at the time, and I had two siblings, an older brother and sister. It wasn't your typical family setting, as there was a lot of tension and chaos that surrounded our family dynamic. Early on, my mother definitely seemed to have some sort of issues with her mental state. My dad explained to me that my mother did not take care of me very well, sometimes coming home to a messy house and my diaper had not been changed for long periods of time. He stated that she was very mean to my sister, as well, who was one year and one month older than me. I fully believe now that my mother suffered from depression, as she had to drop out of middle school to care for her six younger siblings. Her mother was an alcoholic and it got to the point where she could not take care of her children. My mom was the oldest, so she took the responsibility to take care of her brothers and sisters. I have grappled with thoughts all my life whether or not my mother was even expecting me, or if she wanted me. It was obvious she was depressed, and it is very possible she was even using drugs, at the time.

My mother left my dad when I was incredibly young. I am not fully sure why, but my grandmother and my dad possibly encouraged her to give my older brother up for adoption, because he was mixed, half-black. My mother engaged in several affairs while married to my father. She left us when I was one year old, stating to my father that she could not care for us. We went to live with my grandmother, my dad's mother, so she could help him take care of us, while he was working. Around three years old, my grandmother explained to my father that she could no longer take care of us and that we would have to leave. My father returned with my mother, and they got back together for a short while. Our home life was not a loving one, there always seemed to be some sort of chaos and confusion taking place. I was incredibly sad and angry most of the time. It truly makes me wonder if I ever really bonded with my mom at such a crucial stage in my development.

Honestly, the only things that took my mind off of the terrible things happening to me were the fun times I had with my brother and sister. We loved playing hide and seek, and would stay out for hours on end. My mother really did not keep a close eye on us during this time. She would let us stay outside as long as we returned before the sun went down. We loved running up to people's doors and knocking and running away. We also loved going to Market Swimming Pool where you could pay seventy-five cent and swim all day. Me, my siblings, and my cousins could swim like fish. I also remember going to the little corner store called *True Blue*. You could get an entire bag of candy for one dollar. I ate a lot of candy during that time. I loved spending time at my dad's house for Easter. Having an Easter egg hunt with seven kids was a lot of fun. I had two older stepbrothers, two older stepsisters, and a stepsister that was my age. My brothers were really protective over me. These times were truly my solace from the abuse and watching my mother be abused by my stepfather.

Physical, verbal, and emotional abuse by mother took place all my young life. From cursing us out to being dragged by our hair, we endured great suffering at her hands. She would pick things up to hit us with, including shoes and other objects. I understand now that she was only enacting upon us what she, herself, endured not only in her childhood, but also in her marriage and other relationships. My mom was an extremely broken and abused individual.

I did not have a lot of encouragement in the most crucial years of my life. I was held back in Kindergarten because I simply did not have the cognitive support in learning and growth that I desperately needed at that time. One day, on my way to my mother driving me to school, I had a terrible accident. My mother was turning a corner, most likely at a high rate of speed, and I leaned on the door and fell out on the road on my face. My mother rushed me to the nurse's office at the school, but it was more critical than she thought, so we had to go to the emergency room. Luckily, I made it through that ordeal okay, but it has always remained in my thoughts.

Soon after, my mother and father separated again, and eventually, my mom married the man she was having an affair with on my father. He was a very abusive man. He would beat my mother profusely, almost to the point of killing her right in front of me. At one point, I remember my brother swinging around a wooden board that had a nail in it. We were very little and just playing, but he accidentally hit my sister in the head and busted her head open. He was so devastated and sorry, and kept apologizing. My mother understood and knew it was a terrible accident, but my stepfather got extremely angry. He wanted her to severely discipline my brother, but she didn't, as it was clearly an accident. My stepdad told her that since she would not discipline him, he would bust her head open. And he did just that, right in front of us.

Resurrection Fire

Another instance of his diabolical abuse occurred when he was very drunk and on drugs, which was most of the time. He almost amputated my mother's leg by cutting it deeply with a knife. I am not sure of his childhood or what sort of mental state he may have grown up in, but this was over the top. These were very real and *in your face* instances that me and my siblings experienced between the ages of four to thirteen years old. I remember him busting her head open with a coffee mug. There was also a time where he made me sit on their bed in their room while he beat her up. He told me not to move and I had to sit there and watch my mother pummeled by my stepfather. I was traumatized. I recall such pure horror, fear, anxiety, and worry not only for my mother, but for us, as well. I was in fear for all of our lives. This was my reality.

I always wondered why my dad would allow us to remain with my mother and my stepfather. He knew the things going on, but he, too, remarried and had five stepchildren to take care of, and two more would just be too much. He worked two jobs and provided for his family. He grew up fatherless, as well. He was physically abused at an early age and eventually sent to a boy's home. He enlisted in the Army and was sent to Vietnam. There was abuse in his life, as well, so I could understand and see the cycles repeating in my own life, even though he never abused me. I longed to be with him and stable in a loving home. We did stay with him some weekends over the years on and off, and each time we were ready to go back to my mother's house, I begged to stay, and I dreaded it. I loved my mother, but the constant abuse and trauma was catastrophic to my mental state. I must have instinctively learned how to go *inward* as a child. I had to have had some sort of coping mechanism "switch on" upon returning to such an abusive atmosphere. It is utterly amazing what the mind is able to do, even in the midst of such chaos and abuse.

I can honestly say, I cannot remember *many* good memories in my childhood. I know I always desired the absolute attention and love from both my mother and my father. Unfortunately, neither was able to give me what I needed, as one was not in the right mental state and the other worked two jobs when I was between the ages of one and five. My dad had his first heart attack when he was thirty years old, leaving him disabled, and he still had five stepchildren to care for. My early life was pretty much stolen from me. I missed out on my formative years. Instead of being afforded the opportunity to grow up in a safe, loving environment, I was thrust into a hopeless whirlwind of abuse and dysfunction.

You may have experienced something similar in your childhood, whether it was the separation of your parents, physical abuse, drug or alcohol abuse by your parents, neglect, abandonment, or seeing and hearing things a child should never have to witness. You may feel as if you were robbed of your childhood. I want to let you know that you are not alone. I am here to encourage, equip, and empower you to "wake up" and allow the process of healing to begin in your life. What happened to you is not your fault. Hurt people, hurt people, and their pain is passed on to the next generation, but you can break the cycle.

It is absolutely unfortunate that these things may have happened to you, but the most important thing to gain from this evil is to not allow yourself to remain a victim. I had to go through years of counseling and therapy, and I am still going through my own healing process, but I refuse to allow what was done to me to define my entire life. Though I will take you through many more devastating things that took place in my life progressively into my adulthood, there was always a "light" at the end of the tunnel. I have lived through some of the darkest seasons of life, but I always knew, somewhere deep within, that there was going to be a time where the "dead things" in my life would come alive again.

There is hope in Christ Jesus, and I pray as you continue to read my life story, and ultimately my testimony, that you will begin to see the light at the end of your tunnel. Know that your resurrection is coming, and that God desires to use your story for His glory. He wants to take what you went through, and use it to bring someone else out. Allow Him to breathe life into your "dead situations." You do not have to remain in the darkness.

"This is the message which we have heard from Him and declare to you, that God is light and in Him is no darkness at all." 1 John 1:5

Chapter 2

Sexual Abuse:
The Stealing of My Innocence

"But whoever causes one of these little ones who believe in Me to sin, it would be better for him if a millstone were hung around his neck, and he were drowned in the depth of the sea."

Matthew 18:6

I am not fully sure of what happened to me as a baby, or even before the age of two years old. My mother had so many men coming in and out of our home. There were times that she would leave us with men in the church that she felt comfortable enough to watch us, my sister and me. I remember them taking us to get ice cream and buying us porcelain dolls. One of the men picked me up and put me on his lap. He was sitting in the backseat, and as he became aroused, he began tickling me and fondling me. I tried to get away,. but I couldn't. I know now this was absolutely inappropriate, but my mother would always leave us with strangers. Regrettably during that time, I was also sexually molested by one of my stepsisters. She made me perform sexual acts on her and it was very confusing for me as a little girl. These were things you never spoke about to anyone, either because you were threatened, or simply because you were scared or confused.

Before moving to Washington state, I spent time with my Aunt in St. Louis. One of my uncles, my mom's youngest brother, lived with her and unfortunately, I became the victim of sexual molestation by him, as well. My Aunt did not know, at the time, and neither did my mother. I was horrified and afraid to tell anyone. When I finally did, my mother had him committed to an institution. We later found out he was schizophrenic, not that this excused what he did to me, but it did lend some weight as to his mental state. He did confess to the molestation.

In Kindergarten to First Grade, I was sexually molested by my Reading teacher. This was a widely public case, as it was broadcast on the local and national news agencies. I was between five and six years old. The sexual abuse took place in our classroom. He would fondle and touch me underneath of the table, while the other children were right there. I remember him giving me strawberry candy to get me to trust him, I guess. I didn't get candy with my mom often, so this was a treat for me. Unfortunately, it was bait to get me to keep my mouth shut. It was horribly painful, but it appeared to become normal to me because I didn't know. It seemed as if I thought this is what happens when we go to Reading class, as if it were somehow routine. His fingernails were extremely long, and as he would stick his fingers inside of me under the table, it would scratch me and hurt so much.

I found out later that others were also sexually abused by him, along with many other children with learning disabilities that came to him for help in reading. When my mom saw it on the news, she asked me if he had touched me, and that is when I told her everything. I was taken to be checked by a doctor and sure enough, they found the multiple scratches and scarring inside of me. My hymen had been torn, so they knew something had happened to me. Mr. Tansil, my Reading teacher, was eventually sentenced to prison for sexually molesting multiple children. In his first trial, he was acquitted, but was retried in a later case. I have completely forgiven and released him for what he did to me. In the writing of this book, Holy Spirit brought great revelation and finally, after all of these years, connected the dots to my reading disability. My reading disability, later in life, was officially diagnosed during my nursing school program. I had never connected the fact of me not only having difficulty in retaining what I read, but also actually why I hated reading. I am certain that during this time, from Kindergarten to First Grade, the trauma from this sexual abuse destroyed a part of me, and has been a stronghold in my life since that devastating time.

My mother did get me help. The school district paid for me to receive counseling and therapy for the sexual abuse. I remained in therapy and my mother did not follow through with our move until she was sure I was ready for such a transition. During that time, I was throwing up almost daily and always in a state of nervousness. At first, they were not able to diagnose it, but later in therapy, we were able to link it not only to the sexual abuse, but also to the years of trauma I experienced in seeing my mother abused. My hair was now completely falling out, and I was diagnosed with Alopecia Areata, an autoimmune disorder caused, or triggered by, severe stress.

By the time I was in 3rd grade, my mom had to buy me a wig. She told me I could pick out whatever wig I wanted, even though I did not know what type was best for a little girl. Sadly, I was teased and bullied at school because every time I would flip or do a cartwheel, the wig would fall off. I would have to pick it back up and put it on again. It was big and poofy like Dolly Parton's hair. The other kids would get scared because they thought I was contagious, that whatever I had, they would catch. The school eventually gathered the kids in all of my classes to let them know what happened to me, and why I had to wear a wig. This helped tremendously, as more kids were now compassionate toward me and being kind to me.

Children that suffer through abuse carry weights that would be almost unbearable for most adults. I genuinely believe God is with these young children, almost carrying them as they go through such trauma and devastation. All that took place in my life up to this point should have destroyed me. I was definitely suffering many ailments, both physically and mentally, but through it all, there still seemed to be "something" pushing and propelling me to move forward. He was providing me the strength daily that I needed to push through the dysfunction in my life.

"And He said to me, "My grace is sufficient for you, for My strength is made perfect in weakness." 2 Corinthians 12:9a

The vicious cycles in our family seemed almost neverending. From past, to present, and to the foreseeable future, these generational curses seemed almost inevitable. Would we be able to make it through all of this trauma? Could we, in any way, shape, or form lead a normal life from this point? What would it even look like? Could these "dry bones" live?

"The hand of the Lord came upon me and brought me out in the Spirit of the Lord, and set me down in the midst of the valley; and it was full of bones. Then He caused me to pass by them all around, and behold, there were very many in the open valley; and indeed they were very dry. And He said to me, "Son of man, can these bones live?" Ezekiel 37: 1-3a

I want to encourage you that no matter what you faced in your childhood, or even into your adult life, God is able to breathe life into those dead places, into those "dry bones," and create new life within you. Each of us goes through something in our lives, some more than others, but all of us are graced with the strength, courage, and perseverance to make it through, as long as we refuse to give up. No matter if family, teachers, boyfriends, or girlfriends of your parents are sexually abusing you, or even a trusted spiritual leader, please do not keep quiet. Even if you have been threatened to remain silent, find a way to let someone know what has happened to you. Your courage and bravery will not only stop what is happening to you, but it will also stop it from possibly happening to someone else.

Remember, there are many resources available to help you reach out and report your sexual abuse. Whether it is a trusted parent, family member, teacher, school nurse, bus driver, police officer, medical doctor/nurse, school counselor, or even a very close friend, you are not alone. I have provided some of these resources for you at the back of this book.[ii]

Also, seek counseling and/or therapy to help you walk through and talk through your healing process. Far too often, children are told to "get over it" and "move on." I am here to tell you that this is simply impossible! People can, and absolutely do, carry these *demons* throughout their entire lives if left untreated and unresolved. Some may just need emotional support, while others may require more extensive mental, psychological, and even spiritual counseling, and therapy. Seek wholeheartedly for whatever it is you need, and please, do not place a time limit on your healing and/or deliverance. This may only take a year or two for some, while others, it may prove to be a lifetime process. God will be with you every step of the way if you allow Him to come into your life and begin the course of your healing.

"For He Himself has said, "I will never leave you nor forsake you." Hebrews 13:5b

I will deal with my lifelong struggles with sexual abuse and dysfunctional relationships in depth in other chapters. This occurred in various stages throughout my life and certain situations will require a deeper explanation of events. My heartfelt prayer is for healing, forgiveness, deliverance, and ultimate freedom in your life through my experiences and testimony.

Chapter 3

My New Beginning... or So I Thought?

*"The Lord possessed me at the beginning of His way,
Before His works of old.
From everlasting I was established,
From the beginning, from the earliest times of the earth."*

Proverbs 8: 22-23

We finally made the move to the Pacific Northwest. It was almost night and day, as far as scenery and weather, alike. From the Cascade Mountains to the highest peak of Mount Rainier, the mountains of the Northwest were almost magical. Snow-capped mountains and high reaching evergreen trees lined the skyline of Washington state. The brisk, fresh air was unmistakable. You knew you were not in St. Louis anymore. Even the rainy seasons brought such new life and a new beginning for me. Though I enjoyed the new surroundings, I did not want to leave my father in St. Louis. I was going to miss him so much, and miss the peace and stability I had when I stayed with him.

I was now living in Bremerton, Washington at ten years old and in 3rd grade, and they were trying to find a remedy for my hair falling out. My mother wanted to move because there were better doctors in the state of Washington. They came up with an experimental treatment, which consisted of poison ivy. It was applied in a patch that was placed on my arm, which they stated would travel through my bloodstream and reach my hair follicles faster than another treatment. It caused my arm to itch and burn, and it hurt a lot. I was crying one night, and my stepdad got mad at me, and hit me in my arm. I cannot describe the pain I felt, but I let out a huge scream and he got even more angry, and punched me in my head and my face, causing a huge bruise on my face. My mother was so angry. I asked her what I was supposed to do about school and what I was going to tell my teachers. My mother never encouraged me to lie. She told me to tell them the truth. I did, and CPS (Child Protective Services) took me out of the home. CPS would not allow me to return if my stepdad was still there. She asked him to leave. They separated, though still married, and I came home. I believe she was looking for a way to finally get out of this destructive lifestyle.

The court trial for my Reading teacher in St. Louis really took a toll on my mental well-being. It was really tough being held back in Kindergarten. I didn't really notice it much until I began to be bullied by my stepsister and others. I was now battling with a complex of feeling as if I was stupid due to having to repeat the easiest grade in school. People were telling me I deserved the sexual abuse, and some did not believe me, because they thought I was smiling in the courtroom. What they did not understand is that I was extremely nervous to even be there in the courtroom with him, especially that it was being televised locally and nationally. My stepsister not only bullied me, but she beat me up several times. My blood sister also beat me up, as well, due to jealousy during our childhood. She suffered with a weight issue, so she took it out on me. I was getting hit on every side and honestly did not know where to turn, or how to get free from these multiple forms of abuse.

"We are hard-pressed on every side, yet not crushed; we are perplexed, but not in despair; persecuted, but not forsaken; struck down, but not destroyed—always carrying about in the body the dying of the Lord Jesus, that the life of Jesus also may be manifested in our body." 2 Corinthians 4: 8-10

My emotions were a wreck, and my home life did not help it at all. I thought the move to Washington state would make everything go away, or get better, but I was definitely mistaken. What was wrong with me? How was I attracting this abuse, of every form, from so many people? What did I do to deserve all of this? Have you asked yourself these kinds of questions? So often, children that endure so much abuse at an early age can and do carry it into their teenage and adult lives, especially when there is no stable foundation to support you. Yes, I went through counseling and therapy, but my mother was still in very toxic and abusive relationships, of which I became the "secondary abused," being that I lived with her. The sexual abuse continued with a new man my mother was dating; he was actually related to us by marriage. I was about eleven or twelve years old at this time. We traveled back to St. Louis to see our family and he returned to Washington with us. There was inappropriate touching and masturbating taking place with him. I never shared this with my mother; I just kept this inside. I did not know who to turn to, as she was in a relationship with him. My father was not in the state with us, so I felt completely alone and helpless, and at times, hopeless.

"A father of the fatherless, a defender of widows, Is God in His holy habitation. God sets the solitary in families; He brings out those who are bound into prosperity; But the rebellious dwell in a dry land." Psalm 68: 5-6

Father, You protect and help those who can't protect themselves, You redeem injustices through Your unfailing love. Thank You Daddy for helping each person (inner child or inner protected part) who reads this to encounter Your righteous truth and justice.

"He executes justice for the fatherless and the widow, and loves the sojourner, giving him food and clothing." Deuteronomy 10:18, ESV

Resurrection Fire

"But you do see, for you note mischief and vexation, that you may take it into your hands; to you the helpless commits himself; you have been the helper of the fatherless." Psalm 10:14, ESV

Now, I am in middle School and my mother is no longer with my stepfather. She always had a man around, no matter what. There was not a time where some man was in our lives. We lived in the projects area called West Park. I had a few friends in the neighborhood, but only one real friend through middle and high school. I loved school and my teachers, as it was an escape for me from the abuse in my life. Unfortunately, I was always drawn to older men and hung out with the wrong crowds. My mom was finally trying to be a good mom and parent us, but I was extremely angry by this point in my life. I would have extreme outbursts of screaming and crying at the top of my lungs, hitting walls, and being very disrespectful. She was trying to set boundaries and bring order into our home, but it was just a little too late for me. Looking back now, I can see it was a cry of desperation and most of the time, I really had no idea why I was so sad and angry.

I was able to date, even at the age of twelve. My mother did not care that I was with older men I am sure because of the patterns that were happening in her own life. I started dating a man in the Navy. He was in his late twenties, possibly early thirties. This pattern of dating older men began in middle school between sixth and seventh grade. I was sexually active, even from the age of twelve. I was now used to this kind of behavior and my mother did not stop it. I assume because she, too, went through this sort of thing. My grandparents on my mom's side were twenty years apart. My grandmother was of German descent, and it was just a normal thing in those times to either date or marry young, and have children. My grandmother from my father's side was fourteen years old when she married and had children.

There was incest and sexual abuse on my mother's side of the family, and I was the target of this from an uncle, my mother's uncle. Others in our family have also been sexually abused and/or molested. My mother's lifestyle was a direct impact of the sexual abuse in her childhood. I now understand why there were multiple men coming in and out of our home. On my father's side, it was more verbal, emotional, and physical abuse. So, this was a pattern of dysfunction in my family for a long time. It was almost inevitable for me to repeat the dysfunction in my own life. After this experience with an older man, I dated another man who was twice my age. He lied to me about his age, but it was obvious this was a pattern in my life. He even had a daughter. I eventually moved in with him while I was in high school. I was around fourteen or fifteen years old at this time. I was even working while I was going to school. I eventually moved back home with my mother after he began dating another woman.

Early childhood trauma, dysfunction, and abuse scars children and leads them down a pathway of devastation and destruction. Most people you talk to that have had horrible childhoods will tell you that it seeped into every aspect of their adult lives. Many suffer years of turmoil until they are able to get some sort of reprieve either through counseling or therapy. Others endure darkness their entire lives, never receiving healing and deliverance from their childhood abuse. However, there is absolutely help and hope available for us all in Christ Jesus.

"God is our refuge and strength, a very present help in trouble." Psalm 46:1

I share in such transparency with you concerning the abuse in my life because it is a reality for so many all over the world. I know there are many dark times in our lives, and it may seem as if the light will never extinguish the darkness, but it is possible and available to you. I share to let you know that you are not alone, and if you allow the process of sharing your own story to begin, I promise you the journey is worth it. God will use everything you have gone through not only to bring you to a place of healing and restoration, but He will also use it to bring many others out of darkness and into His marvelous light, as well. He will turn around all that the enemy unleashed upon you for His glory and for your good.

"But as for you, you meant evil against me; but God meant it for good, in order to bring it about as it is this day, to save many people alive." Genesis 50:20

Chapter 4

Forced to Grow Up Too Soon

*"Train up a child in the way he should go,
And when he is old he will not depart from it."*

Proverbs 22:6

I was not raised "in" Christ. I went to church periodically during my childhood, but I did not have a relationship with Jesus. My mom would send me to any church she could find just to get a "break," it seemed. I remember being picked up by a neighborhood Baptist church bus in Bremerton. I felt uncomfortable, at times. It seemed like a lot of rules that I couldn't remember. I would clap after a performance while everyone looked at me awkwardly saying I should say "Amen" after someone finishes singing. I was, of course, very embarrassed, and awkward. But overall, I felt safe at this church, and it was fun as a child. I would go to church summer camp and swimming was always my favorite but most of all, I remember the love and hope I encountered.

Dawn Christensen

I gave my heart to Jesus each summer they would have an altar call or rededication service. I would always go running. Looking back now, I'm so grateful. It could have been much worse and I'm thankful my mom gave me that gift. She could have had a break and just left or ran away, but she didn't. I believe it would have been much worse, had my mom not used the Church for babysitting or "child drop off." I say this because I no longer see neighborhood buses or vans going around to neighborhoods picking up kids for church. I also say this because it made such a significant impact on my life that I now realize as an adult, I always picked up family kids or struggling families and gave them a ride to church. I knew if I could just get them to church, or another environment, they would be encouraged and encounter the true Savior. We need to get back to this, as well as home churches and the Book of Acts, breaking bread together and true fellowship with God and family.

"And you, fathers, do not provoke your children to wrath, but bring them up in the training and admonition of the Lord." Ephesians 6:4

The example before me was surely not a healthy or nurturing one, except possibly the times that I spent with my father in St. Louis. The environment I spent most of time in was unhealthy and unsafe for a child. Not having that solid foundation or someone to show me what a "normal" childhood looked like, I was forced to grow up way too soon. My example was constant chaos, confusion, dysfunction, abuse, pain, disappointment, fear, and torment. The path I was heading down was paved out for me by my mother, maybe not intentionally, but it was set before me, nonetheless.

I was barely getting by in high school due to working and not really wanting to go to school. My mother became incredibly angry with me and told me that I needed to graduate high school. I was seventeen years old when I met my first husband. He was in the military and medically discharged. I got pregnant my senior year in high school, but we could not get married until I was eighteen years old. I had a tutor and a nurse sent to my home, so I was able to continue my education and graduate. I turned eighteen in September of 1996, and was married in February of 1997. My son was born in May. I graduated in June of 1997. Unfortunately, while I was pregnant, my husband, boyfriend at the time, began physically assaulting me.

The first instance of abuse, he had gotten his own apartment. He moved from the Bronx to Bremerton, Washington. We were in an argument about me not cooking right and I began crying. He became so angry with me and told me to be quiet. He forced his hand over my mouth, and I was so scared he was not going to let go. I began hyperventilating and got so sick that I threw up. Another time, we were in our kitchen, and he had me blocked up against the wall. He became so angry that he busted a gallon bottle against my body. I was pregnant with our son, at the time. I never knew getting hit with a gallon of water could be so painful and be used as a weapon! He was horribly angry, and you never knew how he was going to react. I was always making excuses for him, even while my family kept telling me that this was not normal.

"Understand this, my dear brothers and sisters: You must all be quick to listen, slow to speak, and slow to get angry." James 1:19, NLT

After birthing my son, I was in a state of post-partum depression. I was so afraid to go home to my husband, even though my mother lived right down the street from us. I stayed most of the time with my mother, even while my husband was at home and my belongings were with him. I didn't move back home with her, but tried my best to be away from him as much as possible due to his anger issues.

Another time, I had my son in my arms and my husband hit me in the head with a high-heel shoe. He wanted to have sex, but I was not in the mood and so tired from having the new baby, as well as being scared and extremely nervous because of the repeated abuse. I didn't feel loved and protected, and I honestly did not know how to be a good wife, either. I did not know how to cook or clean house, as I was not taught these most important aspects by my mother growing up. I was under a huge amount of pressure from my husband in so many ways.

Washington state took a restraining order out against him. In the state of Washington, if there were any signs of domestic violence, they automatically issue this to protect the victim. When the officer came, he could see red, inflamed bleeding and bruising, and the incident had just happened. The officer said it's automatically required and that I had no choice. I originally called in hopes they would talk to him and settle him down. Washington laws were quite different than where I was from in Missouri. I would remember my mom or neighbors calling and police coming but nothing ever happened. I was not protected, and neither was my mother. I realize that Washington law likely saved my life and by the law being in place, I believe it takes a lot of pressure off of the victims. My husband didn't know until much later that it was me who called the police. He initially thought it was a neighbor. I called thinking inside that I didn't want to go through the same thing I did growing up. The torment and trauma had haunted me my entire life, so I thought if we could get "help" for him as soon as possible, it would get better, but this *break* from the abuse was noticeably short lived.

He was charged with domestic violence and sentenced to community service for anger management and ordered to pay restitution. We were separated for at least two or three years, while he was getting better, and he was going to school. This was in 1998. We were separated from 1998-1999. Our daughter was born in August of 2000. I was moving on with my life at this point, and I began dating another man. I was still legally married, but I was divorced in my mind. We eventually got back together. I, too, had to go through domestic violence classes. The restraining order was still in effect until we both had to go through extensive counseling and therapy.

We got back together and moved to Federal Way, Washington. I worked full-time for an airline, and I wanted to be closer to my job. He was a full-time dad and going to school. We were still at poverty level, so he qualified for student assistance. Although most of his school was paid for, he racked up enormous amounts of student loan debt and living this life he couldn't afford.

The abuse returned and it was not only happening to me, but it was now being carried out upon our children. As I worked a full-time swing shift from 4:30pm to midnight, he began to have an inappropriate relationship with a woman he went to school with. It was devastating when I realized the reason my husband was distracted and enacted this abuse upon our daughter. She was spanked so hard that my husband had to put ice on her bottom; the welt was so big, and it bruised. Our baby girl screamed and cried horribly as her father held her down and put cold ice on her wounds. I can't even imagine the terror she must have felt inside.

This spanking and torture was all because her dad overslept and our daughter, about 2-3 years old at the time, had gotten into the fridge and had taken eggs to her room with other ingredients to "make food". I was completely beside myself that her father would warrant such punishment for being a normal, age-appropriate thing to do and all because he was too tired to supervise our kids after being on the phone all night with this other woman.

I didn't report this abuse to anyone because I was in fear for my life, but also because my husband tried to make me think that she needed this punishment, so she would listen. It was shocking to me when I later learned of the abuse my husband had endured as a child. He explained his mother burned his hand with a hot iron to teach him a lesson because he kept doing something and not listening to his mother. He said his mother refused to even take him to the doctor's office. His dad ultimately had to take him instead. She stated that he should have listened to her.

Eventually, my husband threatened to kill me and gut me with a butcher knife. He blocked and barricaded me in a room one night, and hit me with a huge water gun. Our children were now seeing and experiencing all of this dysfunction. I was admitted to the hospital for three weeks for my liver, which caused pancreatitis. He left me for this woman while I was in the hospital and moved into another apartment. I would come home after working and catch them having sexual conversations, whispering. I had no choice but to accept it.

I later found out that his father was unfaithful and had another child (he had a brother he didn't know about). I am shedding light on this because he also had abuse in his childhood and his parents committed adultery/fornication that was never addressed.

The patterns were now on both sides of our families. It was no coincidence that I was being drawn to, and even attracted to, abuse and dysfunction.

"For where envy and self-seeking exist, confusion and every evil thing are there." James 3:16

When I got out of the hospital, I also had pneumonia. Even though our marriage was suffering, I still prayed for healing and restoration. In counseling, he would get extremely angry and even the counselors could see his abuse. He was not only abusive, but really did not seem to want any real help.

The counselor, at one point, told me he was scared for my life and that he believed my husband was going to hit me right in front of him. He was concerned for my safety. I even prayed with my mother-in-law, at that time, for his restoration.

I blamed myself, somehow, for his actions and reactions. This is one of the lasting effects, or impacts, of abuse victims. They will take on the responsibility and accountability for the wrongdoings of their abusers. The counselor said my husband was unteachable and likely wouldn't change given his history and repeated patterns of abuse.

These patterns not only stemmed from my mother and father's family, but also on my husband's side of the family, as well. I almost feel, at times, as if I were "destined" to go through the things I went through, but I now know better. We do not have to repeat the patterns of abuse and dysfunction that our family member's endured, but it is going to take a lot of reprogramming, as well as counseling and therapy to obtain the freedom, healing, and deliverance we desire, and ultimately deserve, in our lives. Unfortunately, this did not happen right away in my life, even after the abuse from my first husband. There is much more I would walk through, but it all is a part of *my story*.

Chapter 5

Patterns of Emotional, Mental & Sexual Abuse

"And do not be conformed to this world, but be transformed by the renewing of your mind, that you may prove what is that good and acceptable and perfect will of God."

Romans 12:2

Of course, the abuse continued. I had not yet received the courage or the strength to let go of these abusive patterns in my life. I always thought they would eventually just get better. I prayed and prayed for healing, deliverance, and restoration in my marriage and in my family, but nothing seemed to be changing. Even when relationships end, we expect those abusive behaviors to end, but what we fail to realize is that though they may have ended physically, the emotional, mental, psychological, and even spiritual scars remain. If we do not face them, they will surely rise up in every relationship we will ever form, and even transfer into our children's lives.

I desperately wished my children did not have to suffer and go through what I endured, or even what their father went through in his childhood. We, as parents, want the best for our children and we ultimately feel as if we can shelter and protect them from these things transpiring in their lives. Unfortunately, we cannot shield them from everything, especially when we have had, or continue to have, dysfunction in our own lives.

Time progressed on and my relationship with my first husband finally ended. My first daughter not only endured devastating abuse from her dad, but then later, he married a woman who was even more abusive than he. I had to get a ten-year restraining order on his wife to protect my oldest two children. So much more chaos and abuse continued after we were divorced; he would still intimidate me. Sad thing is my ex-husband minimizes the abuse to this day, and makes our daughter think she is crazy and that the abuse from his wife never happened. I realize how toxic and brainwashing of a relationship he was in. At one point, I even witnessed her abuse their son and he was in the same room. My daughter was between three to five years old at that time. She would visit him on the weekends for their "weekend custody visits." The abuse my son and my first daughter suffered at the hands of this woman, in this home, was inexcusable. After the restraining order was issued against his wife, he was still able to visit our children. He was allowed to visit with them at my house and spend time with them.

Eventually, I met another man, who is now currently my husband. I became pregnant almost immediately. He wanted me to have an abortion, but I refused. He had a lot of issues with his daughter's mother, so this did not help at all. It was constant rejection, pain, nervousness, and chaos and confusion because he left me in the middle of my pregnancy and was sleeping with other women. I believe the stress of being a single mom in nursing school and him treating me like this contributed to me going into premature labor, as well as other problems during my pregnancy. I had my second daughter, but I was still legally married to my first husband. I had to wait a period of time before my divorce was finalized, as in the state of Washington, an affidavit had to be signed notating the biological birth father before the divorce could be finalized. It is particularly important to be sure that previous relationships have ended, and that you have done all you can do to seal up your past before moving forward.

"Let all things be done decently and in order." 1 Corinthians 14:40

I continued in my education in nursing school and was going to obtain my LPN (Licensed Practical Nurse), and still dating this new man, the father of my second daughter. I would visit him on the weekends as I would drop my other children off at their father's house. He eventually moved in with me to take a pay cut on his job, so he could join the electrical union. We both were attending college at the time. Our daughter was born in 2004 and we were married in 2008. We dated for five years on and off, and got married in 2008 when we both finished school. I completed by RN program at that time.

The relationship with my mother-in-law was good, in the beginning, but once we got married, everything shifted. The first time I met his mother, she completely embarrassed him in a room full of friends. I said, "It's nice to meet you and she laughed saying, "Huh, I know where all your money is going," because I was pregnant. I didn't understand why he would hide from his mom when he went into town to visit friends or his daughter. She would guilt him and he would hide things he bought.

While planning our wedding, I tried to take her advice and have a small wedding that was paid off right away. So, I had one maid of honor and one best man and our children as flower girls in the wedding. My mom began to tell me that my mother-in-law said her, and his sisters hated me and couldn't stand me because they always wanted to be in his wedding. But I had no idea because she wasn't honest to my face as an adult. I was happy to include them in the wedding, but it was incredibly stressful. I had to find dresses and groomsmen and I had to pay for it all. My husband's mom ended up wearing what looked like it could have been a wedding dress. Nothing I could ever do made her happy, and it took me years until I realized it wasn't about me or my kids, it was an unhealthy relationship full of control and manipulation.

In the process of getting married, my mother would tell me some things that she would say about me that were not good. I guess she felt I was not the right "fit" for him being that I was divorced and had children from my previous marriage. She would encourage him to take separate vacations from us, his family. We were both back in church and the men from the church would tell him this was wrong. There was a lot of control and manipulation with his mother. She did not speak to us for over two years, as she was angry with us about the purchase of our first home. She felt we did not take her advice in this situation. She would make him feel guilty and use him against me. There would be times when even my own children would come back from her house and have issues with me. I firmly believe she was not only putting my husband against me, but also my children.

"Hatred stirs up strife, But love covers all sins." Proverbs 10:12

My mother got sick in 2009 and she moved in with us so we could take care of her. I also had to bring in my niece and nephew several times as my sister was dealing with drug addiction. I kept them on and off for about ten years. At one point, I was caring for six children. There was a lot of chaos, confusion, extreme stress, and violence in my home during this time. So much so that I had to get CPS and counseling programs to intervene with him and sit with him while he was asleep, and watch over us due to his violent behavior. I was trying to finally get them the counseling and help they so desperately needed.

Eventually, I had to release them back into my sister's care, so I would not lose my place in the nursing program. My nephew was incredibly angry and abusive. My children were exposed to a lot of abuse, so it was the right thing to do. Sadly, I had to get an attorney to sort out all of these issues in my family. I know now that I took on too much for one person. I have always been one to take on other people's burdens, many times to my consequence. I guess I went through so much in my own childhood that I did not want to see these children go through, as well.

My mother passed away in August of 2011 and sadly, my niece and nephew's father died a month later from liver cancer due to alcoholism. I was so desperate to find out what was wrong with her before she died. I passionately believe she was misdiagnosed. Actually for a long time, I knew my mom was misdiagnosed and I did eventually find a rheumatologist to reassess her case and he confirmed that yes, she was misdiagnosed and that she did not have this rare auto-immune disease. They began to taper her off steroids and the day I brought her home, she spiked the fever from a sepsis infection, but secondary to starving due to malabsorption of all food.

Resurrection Fire

They said it was a rare autoimmune disease that would eat at her muscles. Before I could get another doctor to assess her condition, she spiked a fever and never made it off of life support. I honestly believed that she was going to receive a miracle, but that did not happen. I am so incredibly grateful that she was born-again when my son was young, and we were able to heal through all of the things I went through as a child. We were able to have closure, and I know she is with the Lord.

Through all of the hospital visits, working full-time, caring for five children, and all of the stress coming from every end, I was unfaithful and had an affair on my husband. He was just not present and there for me when I needed him. He was either working night shifts, away on the weekends, caught up in his hobbies, or playing with all of his electronic gadgets and video games. He never had time for me, and I guess this was my way of escape. I am not making excuses, as it was surely wrong, but just trying to bring clarity to my mindset, at the time, and all I was struggling through in my life.

We don't fully understand how years and years of trauma can affect people's mindsets. Both my husband and I endured very difficult childhoods, and when you continue to tack on toxic behaviors without truly getting help, healing, and deliverance, you will find yourself in a pit of darkness, spiraling daily out of control. This is exactly what took place with my husband. I want to touch upon the area of narcissism in regard to my marriage. It played a huge role in the destruction of our marriage, as well as individually in his own life. It not only affected us, but our children, as well.

The Spirit of Narcissism

Narcissism is defined as selfishness, involving a sense of entitlement, a lack of empathy, and a need for admiration, as characterizing a personality type. If left untreated, it can progress into what is called *Narcissistic Personality Disorder*, a disorder in which a person has an inflated sense of self-importance. Narcissistic personality disorder is found more commonly in men. The cause is unknown but likely involves a combination of genetic and environmental factors. Symptoms include an excessive need for admiration, disregard for others' feelings, an inability to handle any criticism, and a sense of entitlement.

Let's look at several other particularly important symptoms to be aware of in the lives of people close to you:

- Have an exaggerated sense of self-importance
- Have a sense of entitlement and require constant, excessive admiration
- Expect to be recognized as superior even without achievements that warrant it
- Exaggerate achievements and talents
- Be preoccupied with fantasies about success, power, brilliance, beauty, or the perfect mate

- Believe they are superior and can only associate with equally special people
- Monopolize conversations and belittle or look down on people they perceive as inferior
- Expect special favors and unquestioning compliance with their expectations
- Take advantage of others to get what they want
- Have an inability or unwillingness to recognize the needs and feelings of others
- Be envious of others and believe others envy them
- Behave in an arrogant or haughty manner, coming across as conceited, boastful, and pretentious
- Insist on having the best of everything — for instance, the best car or office

Unfortunately, my mother-in-law was still very nasty with me and manipulative towards him. She did not even want to see her own grandchild, and this really hurt my mom to witness this before she passed away. We drove two hours into Aberdeen because I wanted to offer for her to see her granddaughter. My husband's sister had to sneak to go to lunch with us, as my husband's mom refused to see her because my husband didn't call her directly. During this same time, my sisters-in-law were genuinely like the younger sisters I never had. I enjoyed taking them back to school clothes shopping, but then during Prom Dress shopping the girls said to me, "Mom said you just used us to get Mike to marry you." I was devastated. It hurt my heart because I didn't understand why someone would tell their teen daughter this. We definitely had enormous pressure from his mom, and I could tell my husband was torn, but I would never make him choose. My mom and my husband were extremely close. There were accusations that I loved to keep my husband busy, so he never had time for them, but when you're raising five kids, their sports, medical, and counseling appointments took a lot of time, not to mention that my mother was dying for two years, and it was a lot of work coordinating between it all. So, when my husband went to visit his mom, she would get furious when I missed my husband. She always wanted him to stay all weekend, but I asked him to come home a little earlier in the evening before bed. I was trying to hold it together as much as I could, but it was just entirely too much to process, as well as handle.

I genuinely believe my husband's mother played a huge role in planting the seeds of narcissism within his life. His father murdered his girlfriend and took his life, as well His mother would not allow him to grow and become the man he needed to be, not only for himself, but as a husband and a father, as well. Every intersection of his life, she found herself right there, making his decisions for him, but they always included what would benefit her, not his own family. All too often, we see this occur in the lives of men that do not know who they are, or their purpose in life. Their lives become wrapped up in their parent's lives, or within the life existence of someone else. They never seem to find their individuality and that they are tremendously important and needed on this Earth. These early abusers, yes, parents that do not allow their children to grow and progress in healthy homes and atmospheres set the foundation for emotional, mental, and psychological abuse in their children's lives. This spirit of control and manipulation at an early age sets the stage for the spirit of narcissism to explode in the lives of adults.

Regrettably, my husband's behavior toward me progressively grew worse. It went from verbal, emotional, mental, psychological, and ultimately to several acts of physical violence toward me. At every turn, I was being tormented by verbal attacks coming from my husband's mouth. Whether I was dealing with physical adversity in my body due to the car accident and all of my subsequent ailments, or struggling through trying to get off my medications, I did not have the support of my husband. All of our interactions were extremely toxic, including our times of intimacy. There were many times he would be very aggressive and volatile when we were intimate. After many sessions of counseling, it was revealed that some of these instances could very well be considered marital rape. He drank a lot and took things out on me every chance he could get. Sadly, he consistently threatened to kill himself in front of us, and one time, I found him unresponsive. This psychological abuse happened so often in my marriage and my children were witnesses to it, as well. I am not sure how we even made it out, as there was so much going on in our lives practically every day.

My husband and I started counseling together again, and I was going to therapy individually, as well. I was on high-dose medications due to my depression, grief, severe focus issues, and mental state. I really had no time to rest or breathe. My life was spiraling out of control. I finally made the decision to go back to church. I desperately needed healing for me, as well as getting my children into a stable environment. We must seek God's wisdom and actually apply it to our lives. The longer we allow these cycles and patterns to continue, the longer it will take to receive our freedom in Christ, and for our healing to begin. We can go to church and pray all day, but until we make the conscious decision to follow His voice, and be transformed by His wisdom, nothing will change.

"My brethren, count it all joy when you fall into various trials, knowing that the testing of your faith produces patience. But let patience have its perfect work, that you may be perfect and complete, lacking nothing. If any of you lacks wisdom, let him ask of God, who gives to all liberally and without reproach, and it will be given to him. But let him ask in faith, with no doubting, for he who doubts is like a wave of the sea driven and tossed by the wind. For let not that man suppose that he will receive anything from the Lord; he is a double-minded man, unstable in all his ways." James 1:2-8

We were getting our lives back and finally gaining some sort of healing for our family, but due to my infidelity in my marriage, he was unable to forgive me and move forward. This was a wall in our marriage, and no matter how much counseling we went through, it was just impossible for him to get passed. He desperately wanted to forgive, but each year around the anniversary of my infidelity, he would become tormented and take it back out on me. It was a vicious cycle. I realized the extremely unhealthy relationship with his mother, who was very controlling and manipulative, may very well have led to his narcissistic tendencies. He dealt with so many years of her tormenting him, as well as our marriage and children. I do wholeheartedly pray for his healing and deliverance.

I encourage you greatly to make a determined decision in your life to break these abusive and destructive patterns. Your life, your children's lives, and those of your future generations depend upon it!

Chapter 6

Generational Curses
The Abuse Must Stop With You!

"... visiting the iniquity of the fathers upon the children and the children's children to the third and the fourth generation."

Exodus 34:7

As Moses met with God on Mount Sinai to construct the Ten Commandments, God spoke very clearly of the sins of the fathers, and the subsequent generational curses that would visit their children and children's children. All too often, we neglect to think that our decisions will affect our own children, let alone generations of children to come. Most people refuse to believe that their actions and/or consequences are only *theirs* to deal with; therefore, they live their lives as if what they "choose" to do ends with them and them alone. Not so.

Our children are like sponges. They see and hear everything we do, and though it may not seem as if it affects them, it does, indeed, not only affect them, but also *infects* every part of their lives, in every aspect. There is an old saying, "Do as I say, not as I do." This is foolishness! Words without action is mere talk to our children. If they do not see us living as we encourage them to do, then they lose respect for us and many times, go and act out in rebellion. When the Bible says, "... *train* up a child in the way he should go and when he is old, he will not depart from it," this extends much further than merely telling a child how to walk and live. To train a child, or anyone for that matter, means to *show them by example*. It reveals that we are living in this way, so simply "watch me" or "imitate me." The Bible reveals this beautifully in 1 Corinthians 11:1,

"*Imitate me, just as I also imitate Christ.*"

Quite simple, yet extremely profound! I had to take an awfully hard look in the mirror and "examine myself," not only in the devastating and destructive patterns of abuse I witnessed my mother endure, as well as put me through, but I also had to come *face to face* with the abuse and destructive patterns I was bringing, some knowingly and some out of my control, into my own children's lives due to unresolved bitterness, anger, resentment, and unforgiveness in my own life, as well as toxic relationships. How could they "imitate" me if all that was coming out of me was toxic and poisonous? Or how could they see the right way, when all they were watching and witnessing was constant abuse of every sort: emotional, mental, psychological, and physical?

There are also instances where children that do not even know their biological parents somehow end up walking out the exact same generational curses, even though they never physically met their parents. The scripture above powerfully reveals this truth, and many people search their entire lives trying to locate some piece to their identity in order to break these destructive generational curses off their lives. Many eventually find out that one, or even both, of their parents dealt with many of the same, destructive patterns in their lives, as well as in their own childhoods. Someone has to make a determined decision in their family, and for their family bloodline, that THE ABUSE STOPS HERE! THE DESTRUCTIVE PATTERNS AND CYCLES STOP HERE! THE GENERATIONAL CURSES STOP WITH ME!!!

Holy Spirit has whispered to me many times, "You are who your bloodline has been waiting for."

Many believe breaking generational curses is not possible, or that it is extremely difficult to achieve. Both of these beliefs are untrue. First and foremost, to break generational curses, we must surrender our lives to Jesus Christ to receive *freedom* from the curse of sin… period.

"... that if you confess with your mouth the Lord Jesus and believe in your heart that God has raised Him from the dead, you will be saved." Romans 10:9

As we make a determined decision to receive His finished work on the Cross for our eternal salvation, we must also make an obvious choice to walk in this freedom in every area of our lives. Whatever does not line up with His Word must be uprooted in our lives. It does not matter if your mother, your father, your grandmother, your grandfather, your great-grandmother, or your great-grandfather struggled with alcoholism, drug addiction, pornography, physical or sexual abuse, or even witchcraft, once you make the choice to submit and surrender your life to Jesus Christ, those curses are BROKEN over your life! You are SET FREE from every demonic force sent not only to destroy your life, and previously in your bloodline, but also your future generations!

We see clearly the Bible reveal curses upon the third and fourth generations of rebellious and wicked people, but we also witness generational blessing released over submitted, surrendered, and sold-out followers of God Almighty. Those who made a determined choice to receive all He had in store for their lives and the lives of their children and children's children.

"And I will establish My covenant between Me and you and your descendants after you in their generations, for an everlasting

covenant, to be God to you and your descendants after you." Genesis 17:7

"And the LORD *said to Jehu, "Because you have done well in doing what is right in My sight, and have done to the house of Ahab all that was in My heart, your sons shall sit on the throne of Israel to the fourth generation."* 2 Kings 10:30

We do not have to accept what the world views as "part of life," or "the hand we have been dealt." We must refuse and reject the *word curses* sent into our lives by either our parents, others in our family, or even words that try to escape from our own mouths. Don't you stand in agreement with demonic and destructive agendas for your life, your children's lives, or of your posterity. Release the TRUTH from your mouth and nothing more! Stand in agreement with the Word of God and accept nothing less! As you stand boldly in the gap for you and your family, you will see the breaking and falling away of the generational curses sent by the enemy to destroy your life and the lives of your future generations. We must develop an absolute desperate resolve to make sure that IT ENDS HERE AND GOES NO FURTHER!

"Set theology aside for a moment. Common sense tells us that behavior and attitude problems tend to run in families. Just like physical characteristics of height, weight, hair color, and complexion. In the same way, certain types of sin can pass from generation to generation. This is particularly true of addictive behaviors such as alcoholism. Similarly, physical and sexual abuse might become ingrained in the psychological legacy of certain families." *Focus on the Family*[iii]

This is fact within my family bloodline, but it is not TRUTH, according to the Word of God. Though we can clearly see repeated patterns in the natural, we have the power and the authority to stop those cycles dead in their path! Having a mother that attempted to commit suicide, it released a demonic spirit within our family (I don't know if there were possibly other family members in past generations that took their own lives). It was a seed planted by Satan himself. I, too, many times battled and struggled with suicidal thoughts, but *something* always guarded me and shielded me from carrying it out. I know God was watching over me, but because I was not aware of how to break generational curses as a young wife and mother, these destructive patterns did make their way into my children's lives. My second husband also tried to take his life. He was heavily intoxicated and had urinated on himself. It still haunts me to this day finding him unresponsive with a noose around his neck hanging in our garage. This spirit of murder, death, and suicide is generational on his side, as well, so it was bound to reach our children, since we did not know, at the time, how to denounce and uproot it, and to cast it out of our family.

My daughter eventually tried to kill herself in her teenage years and again in young adulthood. She also began self-afflicting through "cutting." It was so hard to see this as a mother. I felt so helpless and powerless to protect her. I would like to touch upon also, and be truthful, that there were times when she was older that my parenting, as well, showed abuse patterns toward her, repeating patterns of me screaming and cursing was something I learned from my mother. There were also instances of physical punishment that I carried out on my daughter. These patterns became progressively worse after my car accident. Due to my brain injury, I many times did not know what I was doing. I was unable to control my emotions and would scream and curse uncontrollably. I was not a safe person for my children to talk to, and I embarrassed myself and them often during this chaos and confusion. I am not proud of some of the things I did nor was some of the punishment warranted. These were "learned behaviors of abuse" I carried from my own childhood of abuse and torment. The cycle of abuse was repeating itself and there was no end in sight in my limited perspective at this time in my life.

Sexual abuse and physical abuse ran vehemently throughout my family line. According to the world's perspective, it was "inevitable" that it would continue with me, my children, and their children. Do we simply sit back and receive this *death sentence* for our family, or do we stand up with holy boldness, power, and authority and walk in absolute dominion over the works of darkness? I am, by no means, downplaying or denying the horrible and horrific things that may have happened to you, or your family. I am, however, offering you an opportunity to see what God sees, to hear what He has said, and is yet saying concerning your life and the lives of your future generations. The enemy would love nothing more than to see us continually wallowing in self-pity and ruminating over and over in our minds the diabolical things that we have endured. His desire is to see us bound, in chains, to our past hurts, pains, disappointments, torment, and abuse.

We must make a conscious choice to pull ourselves up out of these dark and destructive places and receive the light of Truth into our lives. This is the second phase of breaking generational curses off of our lives. God offers us freedom from the curse of sin, but now it is our responsibility to discipline ourselves through the Word of God to REMAIN FREE! Most people refuse to think that the places, the people they hang around, or even the practices they continue in are toxic and hindering to their forward progress of freedom. When God identifies, or reveals, a generational curse in our lives, His wisdom exposes the people, the places, and the things we MUST remove from our lives, in order to *get free* and *stay free*. Unfortunately, at times, this may include family members that choose to remain in these devastating and destructive lifestyles.

"Do not be deceived: "Evil company corrupts good habits." 1 Corinthians 15:33

If we are desperate for our freedom, then we will do everything in our natural power, while God works in the Spirit through our obedience, to progress toward breaking free from the enemy's grip over our lives. There are just some people you can no longer spend time together with, there are just some places you can no longer go, and there are just some things you can no longer do. This phase is completely up to us, not God. He has done His part, now it is up to us to maintain the freedom He has freely given, supplied, to us. We must love ourselves enough to *separate* ourselves from that which means us no good, or that which desires to hold us in bondage, or ultimately destroy us.

*"And you shall be holy to Me, for I the Lord am holy, and have **separated** you from the peoples, that you should be Mine."* Leviticus 20:26 (emphasis)

God is separating you not only from people, places, and things, but He is also separating you from the destructive patterns and cycles of your past. He is literally, and spiritually, *severing the ties* between past, present, and future. When God does something, He does it in its *fullness*. Complete restoration is His desire for your life. Though He has, and will, complete this process in our lives, He will use EVERY hurt, pain, disappointment, and tool of torment and abuse you have suffered to bring others out of and into the freedom He has for their lives, as well. Your pain has a purpose!

Chapter 7

Processing Through Your Pain

"Weeping may endure for a night, But joy comes in the morning."

Psalms 30:5

On Friday, December 13, 2013, my brakes failed on my car, and I was in a devastating car accident with my children. I had lost my nursing job a month earlier, and things were changing fast. Coming home that night, I hit a tree. My husband was also laid off work and we were in the process of this car being repossessed. He always said he wanted to fix the breaks himself, and didn't want to give me the money to have someone else fix them. After the accident, he didn't want me to get an attorney, he wanted to keep the car insurance. Obviously, I was not thinking clearly, and he encouraged me to cash in my 401k for a replacement car. I struggled to get myself and two injured children to specialists and therapy. We later lost our house, as well; I was overwhelmed and couldn't keep up trying to find programs, so we wouldn't lose our house. I tried to have it refinanced but we had one overdue payment. If we had an attorney, it would have helped and taken so much pressure off of us.

I was praying as it was happening, and I honestly believe God saved us. I heard the voice of Holy Spirit tell me not to go forward, as there was an embankment ahead of me. This was a 90 degree turn I had to make, and I would have flipped my car, as there was a car at the light. If I would have hit that car, it would have killed this entire family. As I cut my car, we hit several smaller trees and then hit a larger tree head on.

Myself and two of my daughters were injured. My niece was also in the car with us, but received no injuries. I had a severe concussion (they termed it post-concussive syndrome) and whiplash. It later turned out to be a severe brain injury that I have been battling for years. My husband remained abusive toward me, even suffering through this car accident. I had completely blocked out this memory in 2011 until recently. My husband was so upset with me grabbing my wrists so hard trying to drag me off the bed that he abruptly let go, which caused me to bust the back my head on the basement ledge. It was so loud that my aunt visiting us heard it on the 3rd floor. She was furious and stayed at the hospital with my mom. I did not receive any medical care for this injury, so I believe this accident did have some to do with my brain injuries, along with this devasting car accident.

Resurrection Fire

In 2015, I was working at Western State Psychiatric Hospital. I was doing well at the job, but due to the nature of the illness of the patients there, I had to remove myself. Not only was I getting "triggered" due to my past abuses, but there was also quite a bit of violence that took place in these settings. I was having things thrown at me, so I wanted to be sure I was protecting myself against any more possible injuries. I moved to another position at Community Health Clinic, but soon after, I had a Grand Mal seizure due to a negative reaction to medication. These kinds of seizures are typically the result of abnormal electrical activity throughout the brain. I was also having severe migraines throughout this time, having to go to the Emergency Room and get pain medications. I was hospitalized all night and went right back to work the morning after being released. I couldn't keep up and lost this job, no one told me not to go back to work. My husband seemed upset, and he was scared at this event taking place, but never encouraged me to stay home and rest.

I was still working during this time. I kept pushing forward and was not really taking care of myself. From the onset of the car accident, along with a surgery I had to have on my hand which led me to become hospitalized, I believe there was so much stress on my body. My brain was being triggered, which definitely could have brought on this seizure, as well as the severe migraines. I was also being prescribed all kinds of medications for stress, anxiety, and depression. Surely a cocktail for disaster!

Though I was struggling greatly, I knew God will still with me and I knew deep within that He was going to bring me out of this. As we suffer through pain in our lives, whether physically, emotionally, mentally, or psychologically, we must understand that it is not always about just us. As God walks us through our healing, He will, in turn, use us to help others through their pain.

"Blessed be the God and Father of our Lord Jesus Christ, the Father of mercies and God of all comfort, who comforts us in all our tribulation, that we may be able to comfort those who are in any trouble, with the comfort with which we ourselves are comforted by God." 2 Corinthians 1:3-4

From 2015 to 2016, it got really bad. I began to become addicted to the pain medications. It became so bad that I even began taking medications from my family members and friends to get rid of my pain. No one had a solid plan for me to go by in regard to my car accident or the subsequent emotional issues, so they just continued to prescribe medications for me. My women's doctor, after me complaining of hip pain, urged me to get a partial hysterectomy. I was so confused because it was hip pain, I am sure from my car accident. I expected he would go in with a scope or some other non-invasive way to look at my hip, but he was adamant that I get a hysterectomy. I was so desperate to get rid of the pain, so I gave in and allowed the procedure. I do believe God was trying to stop this surgery, as the anesthesiologist backed out twice. He knew something was not right, and normally someone with a hip injury should not have this type of hysterectomy due to being inverted upside down. My husband seemed really upset he had to miss work for the surgery day, and he never took off work to help care for me in my post recovery phase like was stated on discharge. I really needed his help with my medications, but he refused.

I strongly believe I did not medically need this procedure, but money was being made. I told the Lord, once I healed more, that I would go out and advocate and speak out against this miscarriage of medical injustice. I know He wants to supply recompense and restitution in my life due to this medical error. Women are continuing to have these surgeries and are being injured. These are Robotic assisted hysterectomies, and are causing so much damage to women's bodies.

Following the hysterectomy, I began having many issues with my body, including more severe issues with my brain, neck, and lost all range of motion to my already injured hip. Worsened severe uncontrollable pain. I didn't know if my head was hit due to being inverted, but I had never suffered with my room spinning and neck getting stuck or frozen until this surgery. Another thing concerned me as a nurse who used to work in the OR. My woman's doctor tried to do a less invasive cauterization on my uterus while I had an open infected wound on my hand. He said I needed this hysterectomy because my blood was low, but my uterus tilted to the right, so it was not my hip. They should have done the surgery in a lower position, but more money is made in robotic surgeries. There are many articles published with women having injuries due to robots. Dr. Cori, my chiropractor, acknowledges these injuries from this surgery.

Soon after, I developed a severe infection in my stomach and subsequently had an appendectomy. I became very toxic, my urine was Coca-Cola color, and the meds were building up in my body. Later, I would find out, after genetic testing, some of the medications I was prescribed, I was allergic to, and my DNA was severely reacting. I lack the enzymes to clear medications and toxins out of my body. My body was in turmoil, and it was like a domino effect from then on.

In November of 2016, I admitted myself into an amazing Christian facility called *The Center, A Place of Hope* that took a more Holistic team approach in treating where I could receive help for my depression, pain, mental state, and coming off of these prescription medications safely. I did not even make it past the first several days when the hospital called my husband to come and pick me up. They stated there was something severely wrong with my brain and that there was no way my medications could cause this type of damage. Even simple elementary tests performed by the team Psychiatrist and doctors showed that I could not even tell time on a clock. I was even doing things that I did not remember like going into other patient's rooms in the middle of the night. From there, I was taken to Harborview Medical Center to have tests run on my brain. They stated I was fine, and they could not find anything wrong with me.

Resurrection Fire

Eventually, my sister and my husband urged me to take some time away and visit with my father for a while. I did not want to leave my husband, children, and everything I was familiar with and by this time, our home was in foreclosure. But I was desperate to try anything and everything to help me get to the root of my issues. I was in no condition to travel especially alone by airplane because very soon into the flight, not knowing at the time I had a brain injury, I began to have severe head pain and pressure, my heart began to race excessively, and my blood pressure began to drop tremendously. I was not sure if it was the medications or the elevation of the airplane, possibly both, but I was not well. They even considered making an emergency landing to get me help, this was very traumatic. We made it through to St. Louis, and I was immediately rushed to the emergency room. My stepmom and dad were furious. They had no idea of my condition, and I found I had a severe kidney infection and well as kidney stones. I had no business traveling at all. I could not calm my body down and I was in excruciating pain. I had to be hospitalized three times while I was in St. Louis with my father.

Things were going haywire. I found out that the entire time, my sister in Washington was trying to move me in permanently with my father and stepmother. I also found out that my sister tried to steal our home foreclosure money. She had thousands of dollars changed over to her name, and she convinced my husband to scam the mortgage company saying she was a tenant. We were to get the money for moving expenses and for cleaning up the property. She had the check sent in her name; I didn't understand my husband's loyalty to my sister. My son caught the phone call and told me.

My father and stepmother refused to let her follow through with this plan, so I not only felt like my husband and children did not want me, but also my father. My stepmother bought my plane ticket back to Washington, telling me that I needed to be where my support-system was, as well as the specialists I needed to help me figure out what was going on with me. The night before I was to fly back to Washington, I stayed with my stepsister. As I was about to go sleep, everything started spinning. I did not know what was happening, so I asked her to take me to the emergency room. I was freaking out and didn't feel safe to travel due to the traumatic flight to St Louis. She refused and would not even allow me to call 911 from her house. I had to get my luggage and walk out onto the street to call an ambulance. She and her husband laughed at me on the side of the road, and my sister in WA got a "butt-dial" from her phone. It was all caught on voicemail, and this hurt me so bad. Later, I asked why she stated they laughed thinking I was just another drug addict and that they didn't know of my brain injury. This was so hard the betrayal of my stepsister; no drug addict should receive this kind of treatment. It is absolutely inhumane! Anyone who needs 911 assistance should be helped.

As I arrived at the emergency room, the doctors tried to call my family members to corroborate all I was explaining was happening to me. None of them offered any support or vouched for my condition, so instead of admitting me to the hospital to run further tests, I was put in paper clothes and admitted to St. Louis University Psychiatric Ward. I was so scared. They injected me with some sort of medication. They never told me what it was, nor did they even ask my permission to administer it to me. The dizziness and "room spinning" was worse than before, and I remember trying to hold myself up on the wall so I would not fall. The other patients were looking at me strange and I just felt so unsafe. I found out later that it was an extremely high dose of anti-anxiety medication called benzodiazepine that I had never taken before, so it affected me pretty badly.

I'm not sure what the law is in Missouri, but my rights were violated. In Washington state, you must have a court order to force someone to take medication without their consent and being admitted to a psych ward must be voluntary knowledge. This law is in place to protect the patient. I know this because I used to work in Western State Psych Ward. This was an absolute injustice, and I was traumatized. It was like waking up in a nightmare, at times, not wanting to go to the hospital, especially when I have severe head pain and unable to talk or express what's going on inside me. I believe God will give me a voice concerning mental illness and medications. Most are prescribed by unqualified family doctors or even a PA. Another example is when I was in another facility, a Physician's Assistant prescribed me an anti-psychotic to "help me sleep." I had only two days of doses and I jerked and ticked for two weeks.

I had to suffer through this jerking and ticking because a PA didn't even know I was having a rare reaction called Tardive Dyskenesia. This was so painful, my neck and face jerked and ticked. It was traumatizing that I had to figure this out and I entered this facility to safely come off of my meds before entering *A Place of Hope* the first time. I had to do a process of elimination. How can you prescribe meds and not know the severe side effects? It's actually against the law. I know because I had to know any medication I gave as a nurse, again this was a nightmare. I went into a medical facility to detox safely on my own and they ended up doing more damage. It was a naturopathic doctor who I just happened to take my sister to see who told me to go the ER because I was having an allergic reaction to an antipsychotic. Why would they give me an anti-psychotic when I was NOT psychotic? Again, at 38 years old, I never tried marijuana, but it was the only thing that relieved the symptoms. I never got to go back and file a complaint to the PA or Cascade Detox Center. Twice, my kidney had become blocked, and I waited so long because I was scared to go alone. Obviously, I had a tough time trusting the medical system, but my trust is in the Lord.

Going back to the St. Louis University Hospital Psych stay, the nurses did not believe that I was a registered nurse from Washington, or anything else I was sharing with them about my condition. I was there for several days, and I began to have an allergic reaction from the injection they gave me. I had some sort of reaction up my neck, and I was having an extremely tough time breathing. A doctor from the medical facility came through and checked me, and asked me why I was in this part of the hospital. I found out I was supposed to be a medical admit, and not a psychiatric admit. I was devastated! The hospital called around to my extended family, and a distant cousin came to get me out of this psychiatric ward.

"Draw near to God and He will draw near to you." James 4:8

I remember during my stay in this psychiatric ward, I began having open visions of my mother. I wanted to include this testimony to let so many others know that no matter what state you are in, God will be there for you. Even when I was not in my "right state of mind," Father God was revealing that He was there with me. I kept seeing open visions of my mother when she was young, before she became sick. Back then, I realize now, I took on the burden, or lie, that I couldn't figure out her misdiagnosis fast enough. I kept thinking if I didn't have the extra stress and chaos of my sister's children, the violence I mean, maybe I would have figured it out sooner. I knew my mom was misdiagnosed and this was proven finally, but it was too late. I was so blessed to have had the chance to have cared for her.

I was so scared and even my family members thought I was dying, due to the nature of my visions. I was "dying" like my mother due to similarities of our symptoms. The thought also crossed my mind because I worked in Hospice Nursing and I had already seen others that had died, so I desperately prayed and asked God if I was dying. He spoke to me and said, "No Dawn, you are not dying. Check your labs and you will see." He was speaking to me in terms I could understand, not only as a nurse naturally, but as a Believer, spiritually. He told me this was "hereditary" in the medical/natural sense, but a "generational curse" in the spiritual. I actually heard the exact genetic disorder and traumatic brain injury, as well as the medications that played a role. I cried out to the Lord, and I promised Him, "If You help me connect the dots to my mother's death and what is going on in my body, I will NEVER shut up and I will tell everyone who will listen" from what I was suffering. Later, tests would reveal the exact genetic disorder God spoke to me was what I had been struggling to uncover.

Hope is found in the promises God has given us – promises of freedom from sin. We can find so much hope in Scripture through the gift of eternal life made possible through His Son, Jesus Christ. No matter what trials, temptations, or pain we may suffer, we can always hold onto the hope God extends to us.[iv]

My family thought I was crazy and "self-diagnosing." My father was incredibly angry that my sister had the means to help me in my recovery, but chose not to do so, even though I helped for many years support and care for her children while she was in jail and addicted to meth. After she was released, she stayed with us to get back on her feet. This was all very hurtful and disappointing to me, but I had to keep pressing on. I finally flew back home from St. Louis to Washington, and began my new journey into trying to figure out what was wrong with my brain. I had many specialists I was seeing; *Brain Injury Alliance of Washington* was a huge support and connection. The biggest struggle I faced was not having the support at home. It seemed like my husband was in denial most of the time that I had a brain injury. I still remember Dr. Carol Lee, the Psychologist that was seeing our family after my daughter's first suicide attempt, she told my husband somehow your wife sustained a brain injury over the summer 2016. She realized that after my surgeries, I was completely different and displaying symptoms of brain injury. I had lost about 30 lbs over the summer also.

Dr. Carol Lee died in January of 2017 in the middle of helping our family. She was amazing, I had never met anyone like her. She was a Jewish, Spirit-filled doctor who dedicated her entire life to the Lord. She was even contacting family out of state slaying generational giants. I was blessed to attend her memorial service and witness the lives she impacted. I would drive 1 ½ hours to get our daughter counseling, as a mother I would do whatever it took. After she died, my husband seemed upset we didn't get our money reimbursed first. I was devastated and I cried out, "Lord, who are You going to replace her with?" He then brought me Marc Buchheit with *Shelton Healing Rooms* and *Healing the Northwest Ministries* who counsels families, life coaching pretty much anything you have a need for. It was more his heart for the Lord and willingness to listen.

The continual back and forth with me and the issues I was dealing with took our family into a spiraling whirlwind. My husband went through horrific and tormenting bouts of suicide attempts. I was back and forth continuing to abuse medications, even stealing them from friends and neighbors. I found out that I was doing horrible things while in "dissociative" states due to the severe effects on my brain from certain medications, severe pain from trigeminal neuralgia, and brain and neck injury. Stress and pressure put on me from my husband and daughter's suicide attempts, I was many times made to believe it was my fault.

This is absolutely no excuse for my behavior and actions to hurt people and break their trust. The dissociative episodes were later found to happen due to stress and trauma, but the meds and my neck and brain injury also played a role.

I was admitted back into *The Center, A Place of Hope* once again in November of 2017 to help me safely get off of these medications and to get through my constant bouts of depression. There were two doctors that offered my husband a full refund of the treatment if it did not help me. They actually wrote it in a treatment plan. They were fully convinced they knew what was wrong with me and that they could help, but my husband was not willing to do this for me. I honestly think he did not know what to believe because my last neurologist stated that there was nothing wrong with me. Sadly, he went out and purchased a new camera lens for his photography hobby for $5000. I was devastated. This hurt me deeply. My husband would guilt me saying that for his age he had nothing to show. My husband and his mom pretty much say we lost our house due to me even though later, our attorney said we should have never lost our house. I always gave my checks to my husband, and he took care of the bills. My husband had a long time of not paying rent. We lived in our foreclosed house. The attorney asked me where all the money was, and I had no idea. It made me sick to my stomach my attorney asking me if he had a hidden mistress, addiction, or child I didn't know about.

As I was now back at *The Center, A Place of Hope*, I was in therapy six days a week for classes on abuse, boundaries, pain, nutrition, and codependency, as well as extensive therapy with counselors, psychiatrists, and acupuncturists. I was interviewed twice by the counselors and doctor for addiction, but they determined this was not my primary concern or focus.

They were witnessing "red flags" within my marriage, much worse than just cursing at me, but I was brushing it off, not believing he would do such things. I now know I was in denial. He seemed to really enjoy tormenting me. It seemed like it brought him pleasure. My husband was battling through his own toxic upbringing and his own 'demons.' I was so hesitant and afraid to leave my children with him, but I know I needed to get help just as much as he did. It was during this time that I met Marc Buchetteit, a spiritual leader that came alongside of me to help me walk through my healing. He began to counsel me and my husband, and really took on the role of supporting my entire family.

Once I graduated from *The Center, A Place of Hope*, I was now able to see the patterns that were taking place in my life and in my marriage. My husband was in no position to be a support-system for me. He would constantly curse at me, call me names, and tell me he was disgusted with me and wished he'd never married me. I was in such a vulnerable state at this time, as I was only sleeping for one full hour at a time. My blood pressure was so low that my doctor could not even fathom how I was getting out of bed. My thyroid and my adrenal system had shut down, also not realizing, at this time, my neck injury was not allowing me to get adequate blood flow to my brain.

My husband and I went to visit his mother during our anniversary weekend. I was too sick to be left alone, so as we visited her, she actually told me I was a "noose around her son's neck" and that she told him to get rid of me years prior. We visited a Golden Corral for dinner and the extreme pressure from his mother was so much that he stabbed himself in the neck with a wooden skewer. Our lives were pure toxicity! These occurrences sound like something out of a horror movie, but this was my life at that time.

I was introduced to what is called "healing rooms" in my area, and began to receive a lot of prayer over my body and my life. I was also taking natural supplements to combat against the prescription medications I was once taking. Not too long after, my thyroid was completely restored. It was truly a miracle from God and a *ray of hope* in my life, or at least for a brief period of time.

It was now June of 2018, and it was not only Father's Day but also my niece's and daughter's high school graduation day, it was a Sunday. I woke up and my extremities were frozen, my neck, my shoulder, and my arm. I was still not fully aware, at that time, the extent and severity of my neck and brain injuries. I asked my husband to get me to the Church for prayer. I did not want to go to another hospital; I wanted God to heal me. He literally dropped me in a chair and left. My son was so angry, and I was devastated that my children had to continue to witness this abuse and neglect. My chiropractor, Dr. Cory, came in on an emergency basis to unlock my neck, shoulders, and spine. She told me that I could attend the graduation, but to drink a lot of water and eat.

When we arrived at the Tacoma Dome, my husband continued to run ahead of me. I cried and asked him to please slow down. I was in pain and dizzy, and could not keep up. As we went to our seats, my heart stopped beating temporarily. I passed out in my husband's arms. The paramedics came and stabilized me. This incident is really important as it is what led to my legal separation and my husband lying in the court documents. The paramedics said they would transport me, but my vitals were now stable. My husband and my sister promised to take me later if I needed them. They got me home and he and my nephew enjoyed a good laugh, as I paced the floor and couldn't calm my brain down.

I was now at a place in my life where I desperately needed and wanted to be completely healed, delivered, and set free not only from the abuses of my past, but also from the addictions of my present. I did not want to go back to this place. So many women in this program had lived in constant cycles of psychiatric treatment due to sexual abuse and so many other atrocities in their lives. I did not want my future to look like this. My doctors explained to me that I needed to get into some sort of counseling and/or therapy that would help me to walk through my past in order to get through my struggles and addictions. I did just that. My new journey had begun. I was scared and excited, all at the same time.

Processing through your pain can be exceedingly difficult. I not only had to deal with the torment and abuse of my past, but now I had to deal with excruciating physical pain from the car accident, the hysterectomy, and the subsequent shutting down of my body and organs through prescription drug abuse and addiction, or so I thought. My pain was both mental and physical. My torments were both natural and spiritual. I desperately needed to reconcile these struggles within my life.

It was at this point that my doctors were finally getting some answers concerning my health. It was discovered that due to my car accident, and possibly some previous blows to my head, my neurological issues were causing these things to transpire within my body. I found out that my cervical vertebrae 1-7 were stacked on top of each other, so every time I would turn my neck, it would sheer together. Severe neural foraminal and spinal stenosis. I also had a 12-degree curvature in my neck. The severity of my neck injury is not good, and my skull is twisted, so the lack of blood flow has been going on for quite some time and causing severe, at times, out of my mind pain. The c-1, c-2 vertebrae bones are hitting the nerves in my neck, face, and brain, also contributing to me not having adequate blood flow to my brain. My lower spine collapsed, it was supposed to be +35 degrees and it was -15 degrees. By this time, my brain, eyes, neck, and spine were not in sync or working correctly. Most recently, within the last four months, an MRI revealed that my left cerebellar artery and trigeminal nerve are touching. In the medical field, they consider Trigeminal Neuralgia the "Suicide Disease" because the pain is so severe. I had much more damage to my body than anyone previously knew, or were aware of.

I knew something wasn't right after I kept going back. I never experienced room spinning, double vision, or a frozen neck before that inverted surgery. I'm thankful I am better than I was even a year ago.

I was now not only getting hope concerning my physical health, but I was also preparing to receive healing in my mental, emotional, and psychological health through counseling and therapy. Our process is so crucial! Let God do the work in you.

We all suffer in this life in some form or fashion, to varying degrees, but we must hold on to the promises of God to get through them to the other side. I want to encourage you to seek out whatever help you are able to find for yourself, as well as for your loved ones.

"But may the God of all grace, who called us to His eternal glory by Christ Jesus, after you have suffered a while, perfect, establish, strengthen, and settle you." 1 Peter 5:10

Chapter 8

The Importance of Counseling & Therapy

"Where there is no counsel, the people fall: But in the multitude of counselors there is safety."

Proverbs 11:14

We all go through tests, trials, and tribulation in this life. Not one person can say they have it all together. Though we may suffer in diverse ways, each of us will struggle with something, or many things, throughout our lifetime. Many of us were raised to keep our "issues" to ourselves, or within the family. So many in past generations did not share their struggles with anyone outside of the family, and were left to fend for themselves, and in many cases, to tragic detriment. Even in the Church, there was no widespread counseling or ministry to those battling with hurt, pain, disappointment, marital issues, financial bondage, or even physical maladies. Don't even mention emotional, mental, or psychological issues because then you were considered a "demon," and cast out of the Church. Due to this "brush it under the rug" approach, many have succumbed to severe anxiety, depression, and for some, they saw no other choice but to end their own lives.

After finally leaving *The Center, A Place of Hope*, I was seeing several counselors and therapists. My spiritual mentor, Pastor Marc, encouraged me to record the sessions I would have in order to keep a record of what I was being told and also what I was revealing. But most of all, he encouraged me to record the abuse that was taking place at home, so I could keep a record of how my husband made me feel and how he would call me crazy and say hurtful things, saying the abuse never happened. My husband did not believe anything I told him concerning my health or the counseling sessions. At one point, he spoke something so piercing to me. He said, "You are like a rape victim that has never been raped." This hurt me so deeply. I could not understand how he could say such a thing, but now, as I look back, I see that he was dealing with his own tormenting issues. He was not always like this, but as time progressed in our marriage, I believe both of our pasts were being revealed and resurrected. These secrets and abuses had to be uncovered in order for both of us to heal and be delivered.

After multiple instances of neglect, abandonment, and psychological abuse from my husband during the most crucial times with my health and mental state, my counselors urged me to leave him. Not only them, but even my children. My son asked me to get a restraining order against my husband. Our marriage was simply toxic at this point. It was making things much more difficult for me, as well as our children. I even mentioned to him that we could rotate staying at our home. One week he would be there with the kids, and the next, I would be there with them just to give us all a break. He did not want to even try this route, but he eventually left for an entire month. He stated he was living in his van. Our counselors urged him to get therapy for himself, but he refused.

I finally petitioned the courts to see if I could finally get him some help. I was deeply concerned about his mental health, suicide attempts, and the fact that he was going to get these guns released back to him. Unfortunately, it all got turned back on me due to my sickness and mental illness throughout my recovery process. I was at the end of my rope, so I filed for a legal separation from my husband. What I did not know, or our counselors, was that he had already hired a lawyer and was deceiving us all.

Many times, people get married not fully knowing what their spouses endured as children. Unfortunately, these are not conversations that take place before marriage, even though they absolutely should be discussed before making such a crucial decision to spend the rest of our lives with someone. It is very selfish to bring someone into our chaos, expecting everything to "be made whole" simply because we get married. Sadly, we can and will project these destructive behaviors upon our spouses not even knowing we are doing so. We indirectly expose them to our dysfunction, and eventually, they *take on our demons*.

Much has changed not only in society, but within the Church today. There are multiple resources at our disposal. One, in particular, that I would like to discuss in detail is the crucial need for counseling and therapy. It may have been discouraged, or even shunned, in past generations but today, or in the recent past, there are great stigmas attached to seeking out counselors or therapists to assist us in our emotional, mental, and even psychological needs. Let's look at several key components in why people fail to seek help when they desperately need it:

1. Fear
2. Embarrassment
3. Guilt
4. Shame
5. Time constraints
6. Financial obligation
7. Accountability & Responsibility

I have to say I probably struggled with all of these issues at one point or another, but I had to keep pressing in order to get through some of the most difficult seasons in my life. I know I had to talk to someone to get all of this hurt, pain, trauma, torment, and unforgiveness out of my life. Many believe that simply talking to our family members (i.e. mother, father, brother, sister, spouse, or child/children) will suffice, but we must understand that they, too, have their own assumptions, opinions, and perceptions concerning our grievances. We must definitely hear them out, and allow them to process through their own pain, as well. But if we truly desire to get to the root of our own issues, we must seek out help from someone not close to us, and someone that is able to peer into our lives and make a sound, non-judgmental, or biased, hypothesis of what we are struggling through in our lives.

We must let go of whatever hindrances we are facing, or whatever obstacles are in our way, and make a determined and decisive choice to begin our journey towards our wholeness. Don't allow yourself to shrink back due to fear, embarrassment, guilt, shame, or even outward circumstances, such as time constraints and financial obligations. Do ALL you can possibly do to get into some sort of counseling and/or therapy to begin your process of healing. Also, refuse to allow anyone, including your spouse or family members, to project their fears upon you to hinder you from seeking the help you need.

My husband's fear and struggles dealt more along the financial lines, while my battles stemmed from internal struggles. I had to not only push through my inner fears, but I also had to rise above my husband's financial worries. I desperately desired and needed support through counseling and therapy, and God made a way!

There are several types of counseling that you can seek out for help. Here are a few, surely not exhaustive:

1. **<u>Counselors</u>**

- Marriage and family counseling
- Rehabilitation counseling
- Mental Health counseling
- Substance Abuse counseling
- Physical Abuse Counseling
- Child Abuse Counseling
- Domestic Violence Counseling
- Spiritual Counseling

Below are several types of therapists, as well as the issues and disorders they are experienced in:

2. **<u>Therapists</u>**

- **Mental & Psychological therapy**

  ❖ Anxiety disorders
  ❖ Depression
  ❖ Bipolar disorder

- **Cognitive/Behavioral therapy**

  ❖ Eating disorders
  ❖ Schizophrenia
  ❖ Trauma-related disorders

- **Dialectical behavior therapy**

  - Post-traumatic stress disorder (PTSD)
  - Substance use disorders
  - Mood disorders

- **Exposure therapy**

  - Obsessive-compulsive disorder (OCD)
  - PTSD
  - Phobias

- **Interpersonal therapy**

  - Relationships with others
  - Social interactions
  - Negative thought patterns

- **Psychodynamic/Psychoanalytic therapy**

  - Negative thoughts linked to past experiences/abuses
  - Personality disorders
  - Severe anxiety/hallucinative experiences

- **Group therapy**

  - Interpersonal relationship issues
  - Behavioral, learning, or family issues in children and adolescents
  - Medical issues
  - Aging issues
  - Depression
  - Anxiety

- Difficulty recovering from a loss
- Trauma
- Lifestyle issues
- Addiction
- Personality disorders

• **Integrative or Holistic therapy**

- Acupuncture
- Chiropractic care
- Homeopathy
- Massage therapy
- Naturopathy
- Sensory/Imagery therapy
- Spiritual healing therapy

• **Substance Abuse/Addiction therapy**

- Addiction therapy
- Cognitive behavioral therapy
- Contingency Management
- Rational Emotive Behavior therapy
- 12-step facilitation

• **Creative Arts therapy**

- Improve cognitive and motor function
- Improve self-esteem and self-awareness
- Encourage emotional strength
- Build social skills
- Resolve conflicts and distress

According to Psychology School Guide[v], there are thirty-nine categorically diverse types of counselors we can seek out for our counseling needs. You can narrow down the types of counseling and therapy you need from the above lists, or you can research online what is best for your particular situation. Overall, you want to be sure you are seeking out not only qualified counselors and therapists, but you also may want to check their references and referrals. It is always good to do extensive research when choosing someone to share your most intimate secrets and/or trauma.

There is no set structure when it comes to gaining your freedom through counseling and therapy. You can seek out professional licensed therapists, or you may choose the route of seeking out spiritual guidance from spiritual leaders and/or mentors. Depending upon the severity of your issues, this will help you to navigate towards the best possible treatment for you. It is possible you can, and may, utilize a combination of counselors and therapists. However you choose, do all you can until you know for sure that it has helped you toward the threshold of freedom in your life. Another important thing to note: just as the opening Scripture reveals *"... in the multitude of counselors, there is safety,"* be sure to get several professional and/or spiritual opinions, advice, counsel, and diagnoses. You will gain great insight from each, but somewhere along the line, you will hear and see confirmation and patterns of where you are at physically, mentally, and spiritually.

Many that choose the route of counseling and therapy may receive their breakthrough very soon, while others may take more time to get through some exceedingly difficult experiences in their lives. Some may feel that their counselor and/or therapist has helped them completely, and they choose to end their sessions. Others may, indeed, continue throughout their lives in some sort of counseling and/or therapy. Do whatever works best for you.

I have been in and out of counseling and therapy for many years. Due to my physical injuries, as well as my emotional, mental, and psychological stresses (some due to my physical injuries), my experiences may be different from yours and others. I do want to add here that there may very well be instances, whether physical, emotional, mental, or psychological when a therapist will have to prescribe some sort of medication for you. This will only be necessary in more severe cases, but if you have struggled with drug addictions or addictions to prescription medications, you need to be upfront and honest with your therapist, so they can treat you effectively. I battled for years with addiction to prescribed medications, some I should not have ever been given due to misdiagnosis. Treat this with the utmost priority, so you do not find yourself regressing, instead of progressing in your healing process.

The counseling process is much like an educational experience. You can learn more about yourself, as well as acquire new skills. Sometimes, counseling involves learning more about a specific condition (e.g., depression, anxiety, eating disorders) by which you are affected, so that you can better understand treatment options. Below are some examples of what you can gain from personal counseling and/or therapy:

- Improved communication and interpersonal skills
- Greater self-acceptance and self-esteem
- Ability to change self-defeating behaviors/habits
- Better expression and management of emotions, including anger
- Relief from depression, anxiety, or other mental health conditions
- Increased confidence and decision-making skills
- Ability to manage stress effectively
- Improved problem-solving and conflict resolution abilities
- Greater sense of self and purpose
- Recognition of distorted thinking
- Freedom from addictions
- Forgiveness and release from family members and/or abusers
- Healthy relationships
- Self-forgiveness
- Joy, peace, and absolute freedom
- Healing (Physical, emotional, mental, and/or psychological)

I am so excited for you as you embark upon your journey to ultimate healing and deliverance from your abusive and/or addictive past experiences. You do not have accept that this is simply "part of your life," or the "hand you were dealt." You can and will experience freedom if you truly and desperately desire it. GO AND BE HEALED!

Chapter 9

Inner Healing & Deliverance

"For whoever calls on the name of the LORD shall be saved."

Romans 10:13

All too often, we are taught in Church to simply call on the name of the Lord and we shall be saved. This is, indeed, the Word of God and the truth, but what most churches have failed to understand through the life and ministry of our Lord Jesus Christ is that healing and deliverance was the foundation of the Gospel message, and almost ninety percent of the ministry Jesus and His disciples were steeped within in the first-century church. Early in the ministry of Jesus, we see Him going everywhere healing, laying hands on the sick, raising the dead, and casting out demons (deliverance).

"And when He had called His twelve disciples to Him, He gave them power over unclean spirits, to cast them out, and to heal all kinds of sickness and all kinds of disease." Matthew 10:1

Not only was Jesus ministering these miracles unto the people, but He had now given His disciples the power and authority to do exactly the same.

"And as you go, preach, saying, 'The kingdom of heaven is at hand.' Heal the sick, cleanse the lepers, raise the dead, cast out demons. Freely you have received, freely give." Matthew 10:8

The modern church, as well as many past generations, have merely taken on the doctrine of salvation, while neglecting the dire importance and necessity of deliverance. We are leading them to Christ and offering them the opportunity to "believe" in Him, so they can live eternally in Heaven, but is this the original blueprint? Is this the "way" Jesus did it, and is this the "way" He taught His disciples? Sadly, it is not, according to Scripture. Let's take a look at a few definitions to help us understand better.

Salvation is defined as *the state of being saved or protected from harm or a dire situation. In religion and theology, salvation generally refers to the deliverance of the soul from sin and its consequences.* The biblical meaning refers to the redemption of our souls, the saving of the soul from sin and its consequences, including death and separation from God. The Hebrew word "save" means *to rescue.* The meaning of "salvation," Yeshua, literally the name of our Savior (translated Jesus in many regions and nations around the world today).

Resurrection Fire

Deliverance is defined as *the action of being rescued or set free*. The biblical meaning refers to the act of delivering someone or something: the state of being delivered especially: liberation, rescue. The word "liberation" simply put, means *freedom*. The Hebrew word "deliverance" means the same as salvation, the name Yeshua. A quick sidenote here: salvation and deliverance can only come through Yeshua (Jesus). It cannot be wrought by or through the hand of mere man. It is something supernaturally imparted from an infinite God to finite man. Though these two words are remarkably similar in nature, they are incredibly unique in context and concept, as it pertains to the deliverance of mankind from oppression, sickness, disease, and yes, demonic influence in the Earth realm. We are "saved to" eternal life with our Creator through the shed blood of Christ on the Cross, but what about those things that torment and torture us in our mind, body, soul, and spirit?

How often do we see people go to church, receive the call to salvation, go to the front to rehearse what the pastor tells them to say, and then they believe they are saved and going to Heaven? They assume all will be immediately fixed and changed in their lives. This is not all of their fault, as so many pastors refuse and reject to teach on inner healing and deliverance. There are many reasons why this is so. One, fear. Yes, unfortunately many pastors are fearful of casting out demons. They will preach concerning it from the Word of God, but not practice it within their churches. Secondly, unbelief. Some pastors do not even believe in the demonic, even though it is clearly revealed in

Scripture. Finally, and probably the most disturbing, control, manipulation, and ultimately, monetary gain. Many pastors refuse to teach on and incorporate inner healing and deliverance within their churches, because they simply do not desire the deliverance of people. We are witnessing this increasingly in today's church culture. Pastors would rather the people under their covering remain in bondage, so that they can manipulate and control them through these demonic states of bondage. They lure people in through idol worship, and they remain in torment in every area of their lives. Sadly, many pastors are not delivered themselves, and never have been. This is an epidemic within today's Church.

His desire is to heal AND deliver His people.

"He heals the brokenhearted and bandages their wounds."
Psalm 147:2

After so many battles back and forth in court with the separation between me and my husband, and with the constant attacks and spiritual warfare in my mind and body, it seemed as if nothing was going to change in my life. There would be times of great breakthrough, then more battles would come up in my life. The counseling and therapy was always a reprieve from my day-to-day struggles, but I needed absolute breakthrough! In August of 2018, I went to a healing conference called *Compassion Action* with Chris Overstreet. I had the most amazing encounters at this conference, including being baptized with laughter. I had never experienced anything like this in my entire life. God even used me to pray for a blind man in this meeting. He was born a hermaphrodite, and his parents chose his gender for him. He was dressed and living as a woman.

During the time I was interceding and praying for him, God revealed what his intended and created gender was to be. I explained to him what God was saying to me, and he was moved deeply by Holy Spirit. The divine connection was undeniable as to why God had me, of all people, to go and pray for him. We both had severe childhood traumas, and surprisingly, he also had a remarkably similar surgery that I had, as well. As we were praying for him, there were two other women with us and we began to break these things off of his life, his vision went from black, to gray. He was receiving partial sight right there! I told him that God does not start what He will not finish, so if He was going to heal him in this conference, on his way home, or progressively, it was going to come to pass! I was believing for this man's inner healing and deliverance even desperately needing it myself!

I was also delivered from the fear of man in this conference. On my way driving to this conference in Oregon with several friends, I was having terrible headaches and migraines. The supernatural presence of God completely enveloped my entire body and healing manifested in so many ways. I was the first person in the lines each day, and one of the last to leave. I did not want to leave because His presence was so beautiful. I continued to press on after leaving, even though I was still in a not so good place in my life. I was on a healing journey, and I could not allow anything to hinder what God was doing in my life. I left most of the medical system due to the negligence of doctors misdiagnosing me. I may not have seen it immediately, but He was working behind the scenes. I had no other choice but to trust Him.

"My son, give attention to my words; Incline your ear to my sayings. Do not let them depart from your eyes; Keep them in the midst of your heart; For they are life to those who find them, And health to all their flesh." Proverbs 4: 20-22

At this point, God was leading me every step of the way. I had to rely upon His voice to guide me through all of this, because I simply could no longer trust the medical community. It has been such a long journey, but nothing and I mean absolutely nothing could separate me from Him. I knew He could be trusted.

"Who shall separate us from the love of Christ? Shall tribulation, or distress, or persecution, or famine, or nakedness, or peril, or sword?" Romans 8:35

There were miracles happening all throughout this time. I had received my medical disability funding from the federal government for working so long as a Registered Nurse. *The Brain Injury Alliance of Washington* helped me to process the disability on the first attempt. This is almost unheard of. God was showing me favor everywhere I went. I would go to appointments and sit for hours, but there was always someone there He wanted me to pray for. It was truly supernatural. I did not know much about prophetic ministry, I was not taught it, but somehow, He was using me in this exact capacity in others' lives. He also told me not to hire an attorney that He was going to be my Attorney from here out. He was literally walking with me every step of the way. I was learning that He knew exactly what I had been through, was going through, and anything that I would go through in the future. He knows us intimately, and He has been there.

"He took up our pain and bore our suffering, yet we considered Him punished by God, stricken by Him and afflicted. But He was pierced for our transgressions, He was crushed for our iniquities; the punishment that brought us peace was on Him, and by His wounds, we are healed." Isaiah 53:5

We must be able to fully understand even the distinct differences and "processes" between *Inner healing* and *Deliverance*. We have to allow the work of Holy Spirit to uncover and reveal things hidden deep within our hearts and minds, those things we may have pushed down within that we did not want to remember, or we may have blocked out due to childhood traumas in our lives. Many people cannot even fully remember some of the things that happened to them due to such horrific experiences. As we submit to allowing not only Holy Spirit, but those gifted in Inner Healing and Deliverance, to help us walk through these past traumas, this opens the door for our healing to begin. This process can be immediate for some, and for others, much longer. Whatever your process, continue until you receive your breakthrough! Simply put, the breakthrough is your Deliverance!

Let's look at some areas that may hold us back from receiving our healing:

1. Anger/Hatred
   - "Be angry, and do not sin, do not let the sun go down on your wrath, nor give place to the devil." Ephesians 4:26-27

2. Unforgiving/Relentless
   - "And whenever you stand praying, if you have anything against anyone, forgive him, that your Father in heaven may also forgive you your trespasses." Mark 11:25

3. Bitterness/Resentment
   - "Let all bitterness, wrath, anger, clamor, and evil speaking be put away from you, with all malice." Ephesians 4:31

4. Rage/Wrath
   - "He who is slow to wrath has great understanding,
     But he who is impulsive exalts folly." Proverbs 14:29

5. Self-pity/Lack of Gratitude/Victimization
   - "I have told you these things, so that in me you may have peace. In this world you will have trouble. But take heart! I have overcome the world." John 16:33

6. Unbelief/Doubt
   - "Beware, brethren, lest there be in any of you an evil heart of unbelief in departing from the living God." Hebrews 3:12

7. Vengeance/Grudges
   - "You shall not take vengeance, nor bear any grudge against the children of your people, but you shall love your neighbor as yourself: I am the Lord." Leviticus 19:18

8. Sin/Disobedience
   - "But your iniquities have separated you from your God; And your sins have hidden His face from you, So that He will not hear." Isaiah 59:2

One of my greatest struggles was not being able to forgive. It was hard for me to continue walking in forgiveness, even on a daily basis. Things would easily trigger my anger, and I would take it out on everyone else. My family had pretty much lost all grace for me after my accident. I know it could not have been easy for them having to go through all they went through during my times off struggle, but the enemy continued ravaging my thoughts. I know some of it was brought on by the multiple medications I was taking. I literally was not in my right mind. I guess the unforgiveness stemmed from my own self-pity. I knew deep within that God was with me and that He would never leave me or forsake me, but I have to be honest, I could not seem to find that place of gratefulness. I could not understand why all of these things continued to happen to me. I questioned God a lot, and I just wanted my family to somehow understand how I was suffering. I finally realized that they were suffering, too.

Trauma in one person's life does not simply affect them, it can and will affect their marriage, their children, their family members, and honestly anyone close to them. It is surely not what I wanted or desired for my family, but one thing we have to fully grasp is that "no matter what" any of us go through, no matter how difficult our situations may be, we MUST stand with our loved ones that are suffering, and seek God wholeheartedly to help us to endure and persevere through the challenging times.

For me, it was a battle to receive my emotional, mental, and psychological healing (inner healing), due to the extreme pain I suffered through daily. I believe I was not only angry with my family, but in some ways with God, as well. I know we do not like to admit this and be transparent in this capacity, but God is more than able to handle the truth in our lives, and honestly, demands and commands it from us, so we can walk in absolute freedom. It is in this place of truth where our healing will begin to manifest in our lives. We must be willing to cry out in pure truth and transparency, and He will hear us and heal us from our troubles. But we must also be sure that we have surrendered any hurt, unforgiveness, anger, bitterness, self-pity, and any sin in our lives over to Him.

"The righteous cry out, and the Lord hears, and delivers them out of all their troubles." Psalm 34:17

All throughout Scripture, we can clearly see Father God delivering His people out of bondage, oppression, slavery, persecution, sickness, disease, and demonic possession and oppression.

"Heal me, O Lord, and I shall be healed; save me, and I shall be saved, for you are my praise. For I will restore health to you, and your wounds I will heal, declares the Lord. Behold, I will bring to it health and healing, and I will heal them and reveal to them abundance of prosperity and security." Jeremiah 17:14-16

This particular scripture in Jeremiah gives distinction between healing, deliverance, and salvation. We must understand they are separate manifestations of His grace and mercy. There is too much evidence that reveals the lack of one, or several of these occurrences, in the lives of professing born-again Believers in Christ Jesus. Far too often, we are witnessing church going, Bible-believing people entangled in sin and bound with demonic strongholds in their lives, marriages, children, and many other areas. This should not be so.

We must get back to the foundations of the Gospel and follow the blueprint that Jesus provided for us to gain freedom

(Inner Healing and Deliverance) here in the Earth. He would never want us merely saved to go to Heaven one day, yet remain bound in this sphere of space and time. Yes, there are things we will surely suffer through as we continue to follow Him, and also the things we will simply go through in this world, but our Father is not sadistic. It is CLEAR that His desire is to set us free not only to eternity in the afterlife, but here on Earth, as well.

As you receive your inner healing from past traumas and breakthrough in deliverance from anything that has held you in bondage, it is now time to fill yourself up with the Word of God, be filled with Holy Spirit, and to guard yourself against any tormenting spirits that may try to return into your life. Yes, this is absolutely possible. Let's look at this scripture:

"When an unclean spirit goes out of a man, he goes through dry places, seeking rest, and finds none. Then he says, 'I will return to my house from which I came.' And when he comes, he finds it empty, swept, and put in order. Then he goes and takes with him seven other spirits more wicked than himself, and they enter and dwell there; and the last state of that man is worse than the first." Matthew 12:43-45

Don't allow yourself to become "empty" after you go through Inner Healing and Deliverance. The Word of God provides us with strategic wisdom in order to remain free from the traps of the enemy. Here is some final wisdom to get free and stay free!

"Finally, my brethren, be strong in the Lord and in the power of His might. Put on the whole armor of God, that you may be able to stand against the wiles of the devil. For we do not wrestle against flesh and blood, but against principalities, against powers, against the rulers of the darkness of this age, against spiritual hosts of wickedness in the heavenly places. Therefore take up the whole armor of God, that you may be able to withstand in the evil day, and having done all, to stand." Ephesians 6:10-13

Here are the seven pieces of the Armor of God that we must cover ourselves in daily to remain guarded against the tactics of our enemy:

- The Belt of Truth
- The Breastplate of Righteousness
- The Gospel of Peace
- The Shield of Faith
- The Helmet of Salvation
- The Sword of the Spirit
- Prayer

Read and meditate on Ephesians 6:14-18 thoroughly and allow God to process and prepare you to stand against the spiritual attacks on your life:

"Stand therefore, having girded your waist with truth, having put on the breastplate of righteousness, and having shod your feet

with the preparation of the gospel of peace; above all, taking the shield of faith with which you will be able to quench all the fiery darts of the wicked one. And take the helmet of salvation, and the sword of the Spirit, which is the word of God; praying always with all prayer and supplication in the Spirit, being watchful to this end with all perseverance and supplication for all the saints—"

Spiritual healing and deliverance is available to everyone who sincerely calls upon the name of the Lord. And there are many sources of professional and spiritual assistance for those who need practical help—pastors, therapists, counselors, and doctors. I have included a Resource page at the end of the book with websites and phone numbers you can utilize along your journey to freedom!

"He has delivered us from the power of darkness and conveyed us into the kingdom of the Son of His love, in whom we have redemption through His blood, the forgiveness of sins." Colossians 1:13-14

Chapter 10

Lazarus... Come Forth!

"Now when He had said these things, He cried with a loud voice, "Lazarus, come forth!" And he who had died came out bound hand and foot with graveclothes, and his face was wrapped with a cloth. Jesus said to them, "Loose him, and let him go."

John 11: 43-44

In May of 2020, in the midst of the quarantine, Father God showed Himself mighty in my life. Even from 2018 until the present, I have been healing progressively not only in my heart, mind, soul, and spirit, but also in my body. I am not where I was ten years ago, and I am not where I was even a year ago. I was led back to a previous doctor by the Lord, and it was truly God-breathed. It was an absolute divine set-up for the both of us. In the midst of him treating me, God gave me a word of knowledge for his wife. Once again, what we go through is not always simply about us. God will use even our times of struggle to minister to someone else. I am so incredibly grateful to be used, even in my own pain. He truly receives all the glory.

During this time, God also opened many doors for me to grow spiritually and to receive much help and assistance through my process of Inner Healing and Deliverance. I have learned so much about myself and about God's unconditional love for me. Not only am I receiving spiritual support and newfound medical treatments, but He has provided for me financially beyond anything I could have ever imagined. I am making just as much money as I did as a Registered Nurse, but now I am able to be at home receiving the much need rest, medical care, and peace I should have taken when I had the accident.

God also blessed me with a wonderful home here in Washington beyond my dreams. It is a beautiful cottage in a breathtaking area that brings so much peace into my life. It was truly His favor, as it was not even on the market for three years. In 2019, I sowed the largest seed I had ever sown, just thanking God for His goodness in my life. In January of 2020, I was able to purchase a Bemer machine, which is an electromagnetic frequency that sends waves to stimulate the muscles and to increase blood circulation. The physical vascular care has improved my life tremendously. I desired to purchase one years ago, but was unable due to financial strains. God is such a good God! Not only was this providing me with a better quality of life, but since last year, He has opened the door for me to offer this service to so many others suffering through pain and health issues. It is providing me the opportunity to minister the love of God to so many people. I could have never imagined God would use my pain to bring about such healing, deliverance, and joy in the lives of others.

I have lost so much in my lifetime, including my marriage and even my children to an extent. They suffered through so much over the years watching me go through tremendous dysfunction, trauma, pain, addiction, confusion, and chaos. So much of what I endured was indirectly, and sometimes directly, placed upon them when it should not have been. I pray one day they are able to heal and be delivered from all they have endured, and know that I never wished this upon them. I pray they will find it in their hearts to forgive me. Throughout the entire pandemic of 2020, I was mostly alone in my home. Though I felt alone many times, and cried out to God in desperation, I can look back now and see how He was moving in my life. He was processing, preparing, and positioning me for my healing and deliverance. I could no longer blame anyone, and I had to take an awfully long look in the mirror of my own life and take accountability and responsibility for me! I had to get rid of the self-pity and self-destructive patterns I was used to and allowing myself to become entangled within for so many years. I had to allow God to break me, so that the chains could be broken over my life.

During this time in isolation, I had to truly let go of everything and everyone and let Him transform my life! Even if I never reconciled with my husband and even if my children walked away from me, I had to gather in my heart that no matter who left me and no matter what I lost, God Himself would restore, renew, refresh, redeem, reconcile, and RESURRECT MY LIFE FOR HIS GLORY!!! His desire was to "make all things new!"

"So Jesus answered and said, "Assuredly, I say to you, there is no one who has left house or brothers or sisters or father or mother or wife or children or lands, for My sake and the gospel's, who shall not receive a hundredfold now in this time— houses and brothers and sisters and mothers and children and lands, with persecutions—and in the age to come, eternal life."
Mark 10:29-30

I have been watching Him do this before my very eyes! He has brought some of the most beautiful and compassionate people into my life. People who have spoken pure life into me, and who have walked alongside of me, holding my hand and my heart. And then there are some that refused to allow me to wallow in shame, guilt, pity, and condemnation of myself. These precious people have literally "pulled me from the flames of hell!" Then, there are those that have poured and sowed healing and deliverance like *water on these dry bones.*

I am feeling and sensing the call to "come forth" out of the grave, just as Lazarus! For so many years, I felt as if I was buried alive. To imagine being buried in a coffin with no room to move,

Resurrection Fire

darkness beyond comprehension, very little oxygen to breathe, and just waiting to take that last breath not knowing for sure which side of eternity I would find myself. I felt helpless and hopeless for so many years. I often wondered if I would ever be "pain free," or emotionally and mentally stable. I processed over and over in my mind the atrocities committed against me as a child, in my marriages, and from my family members. I blamed myself for things that were not my fault, and attributed my abuse, sexual violations, car accident, my failed marriages, and my physical impairments with the "judgment" of God upon me. I was blinded by the enemy of my soul! BUT GOD… He was, and yet is, calling me, "DAWN… COME FORTH!!! He is calling you, as well!

"For the believer, there is hope beyond the grave, because Jesus Christ has opened the door to heaven for us by His death and resurrection. *~Billy Graham*

For so many years, I wondered and questioned God, "Why, God? Why would You allow all of this pain, abuse, and suffering in my life?" Now, on the other side, I can understand better. My blinded eyes are opening, and my deaf ears can hear His voice clearer. Yes, I was buried in that grave, and yes, I did die… I died to my past. I died to my pain. I died to my pity. I died to *my flesh*.

Dawn Christensen

"That I may know him, and the power of his resurrection, and the fellowship of his sufferings, being made conformable unto his death." Philippians 3:10

I was reminded of His death. I had to come 'out of myself' for a season, in order to remember my Lord and His sufferings. We, as children of God, are partakers of His sufferings. Nowhere do we see in the Word of God where we are free from pain, tests, trials, and tribulation in this life. In fact, we are guaranteed such if we commit and surrender our lives to Him. We are *conformed to His death*, so we are able to walk with Him in greater understanding, knowledge, wisdom, revelation, and ultimately, intimacy. We are called to be transformed into His image and buried with Him, so we can be raised with Him.

"Therefore we were buried with Him through baptism into death, that just as Christ was raised from the dead by the glory of the Father, even so we also should walk in newness of life." Romans 6:4

I can attest of this "newness of life," as everything was changing around me. In December of 2019, I attended a "Raising the Dead" conference with David Hogan. I had an open vision of doing ultrasounds to show the beauty of life to a world trying to destroy it. That was on a Monday. By Wednesday, I attended a Bible Study, and I met a woman that works in this field. My body lit up like a Christmas tree! I knew in my spirit that this was a confirmation from the Lord. I wasn't sure whether I was supposed to pray for her, intercede, or if God was leading me in this direction. She revealed she with worked with Care Net Pregnancy & Family Services Ministry Abortion Recovery Program. God was taking away all of my excuses as to why I could not do ultrasounds. I did not know how to do them, and I was not licensed to do this. They told me they would teach me for free. I now do this every Wednesday to earn hours toward my nursing license, as I continue to heal and go to therapy. Our Father is so faithful!

I am still currently in therapy, and I am confident that the Lord will finish what He started in me. The full financial obligation for my therapy was raised, and my doctor, Dr. Leone, has written off the entire payment for my lower spine. This was truly a divine appointment from God. I am keenly aware that my healing will be progressive as I grow and walk with Him even greater and deeper in intimacy. I love being in His presence and fellowshipping with Holy Spirit. I love growing deeper and deeper in love with my Savior. I am truly being made new, and every dead thing in my life is coming alive once again! The RESURRECTION FIRE is burning deep within me, and I am in great expectation of all He will continue to do in and through my life for HIS GLORY! I am also extremely excited for you and the great testimonies that will come out of the "dead places" of your life, as well. Trust Him, and allow the *Resurrection Fire* of the Lord to purge and purify you and make all t*he dead things in your life to be made alive again*!

Conclusion

Life happens to us all. My story may be uniquely different from yours, but each of us has a narrative to convey and communicate to the world. No matter what you have gone through in your life, from your childhood and even into adulthood, it does not have to be the end of your story. What happened to you does not define you. What you endured, God can and will use for His ultimate glory if you submit and surrender all of your pain, trauma, and abuse over to Him. I share in transparency so that others can know they are not alone. Far too often, we are encouraged to suppress our childhood traumas and to move on with our lives. We are told to "forgive and forget." This is just simply not possible. We must deal with the things that have negatively impacted our lives, so that we are able to be healed, delivered, and set free to live productive lives.

Your process of healing and deliverance has the capacity to not only transform your life, but it has the ability to shift entire generations. Don't be afraid to allow vulnerability to take place in your life. As you surrender your deepest and darkest secrets to God, He is able to do exceedingly, abundantly above all you could ever ask or think. Your testimony has the power to help so many others out of their darkness, as well. Choose to break free from the bondage of your past, throw off the "grave clothes," "come out of your tomb," and allow the RESURRECTION FIRE of God to lift you to life everlasting in His holy presence!

Resources

1. **National Suicide Prevention Lifeline**: Phone: 1-800-273-TALK (8255)

   Lifeline Chat: Lifeline chat is a service of the National Suicide Prevention Lifeline, connecting individuals with counselors for emotional support and other services via the web chat. All chat centers in Lifeline network are accredited by CONTACT USA. Lifeline chat is available 24/7 across the U.S.

   https://suicidepreventionlifeline.org

2. **Crisis Text Line**: Text HOME to 741741 from anywhere in the United States, anytime. Crisis Text Line is here for any crisis. A live, trained Crisis Counselor receives the text and responds, all from their secure online platform. The volunteer Crisis Counselor will help you move from a Hot moment to a Cool moment. Get help today for Coronavirus, Anxiety, Eating Disorders, Depression, Suicide, Self-Harm.

   US: Text 741741

   CA: Text 741741

   UK: Text 85258

   Ireland: 50808

3. **YWCA:** largest network of domestic and sexual violence service providers in the nation offers emergency, transitional, and long-term housing, crisis hotlines, medical and legal advocacy, and other services to survivors of domestic and sexual violence survivors can regain stability and as they rebuild their lives.

   https://www.ywca.org/
   Phone: (202) 467-0801

4. **Healing the Northwest & International Ministries**: Skilled team in ministering Jesus… His love, goodness, grace, joy, and healing for all physical, mental, or emotional needs. Discover your true identity and destiny in Jesus Christ.

   You can set up phone or in-person appointments for pastoral counseling, life coaching, healing prayer, inner-healing or prophetic ministry.

   Text or Call (360)-490-4948 or book online:

   https://healingthenw.com

5. **Focus On the Family Christian Counselors Network:** https://www.focusonthefamily.com/get-help/counseling-services-and-referrals/.

6. **SAMHSA National Helpline (Substance Abuse):** 1-800-662-4357

7. **Person-Focused Vet Programs - Evidence-Based Addiction Rehab (Military Veterans):**
   https://www.belairerecovery.com (888) 202-5046

8. **Lion's Light International**: Inner Healing & Deliverance Ministry https://www.lionslightinternational.org.

9. **Domestic Abuse Hotline:** National Domestic Violence Hotline (NDVH) is a 24-hour confidential service for survivors, victims and those affected by domestic violence, intimate partner violence and relationship abuse. ADVOCATES are available at

    1-800-799-SAFE and through online chatting at:
    www.TheHotline.org
    All calls and chatting is FREE and confidential.

10. **Mercy Multiplied International** is Restoring Hope and Transforming and is a nonprofit Christian organization that equips people to live free and stay free through Jesus Christ. They offer multiple programs and resources online and onsite.

    (615)831-6987
    info@mercymultiplied.com
    https://mercymultiplied.com

Prayers

Father God, I pray for every reader that touches this book that You would reveal Yourself unto them. Use my life as a living testimony of Your goodness and faithfulness to heal, deliver, renew, restore, redeem, and resurrect for Your glory. Heal the deep, broken places in their lives and draw them into Your precious presence, so they will know Your magnificent love for them. Bring Your peace to their hearts, so they can receive closure of their pasts and forgive those that have caused so much pain and hurt in their lives.

I pray for those that have suffered through childhood abuse and trauma. Lord, touch those secret places that so many suppress and keep hidden for so many years. Holy Spirit, release them from the guilt and shame associated with their abuse and heal them and deliver them from torment. Set them free so they can be all You created them to be in this life.

Father, I pray for anyone suffering through addictions, whether it be medical prescriptions, drugs, alcohol, and any and all sexual addictions related to physical or sexual abuse in their childhoods, or even adult lives. We believe for a complete and restorative healing in their lives, both naturally and spiritually.

Dawn Christensen

I pray for children of adult traumas, those that have had to grow up in toxic homes witnessing verbal, emotional, mental, psychological, physical, and sexual abuse of their parents and/or guardians. Father, heal and deliver these children from these traumas and let them know that it was not their fault and that they were not the reasons these things took place. Release them from these diabolical burdens sent to destroy their lives. We believe in the resurrection power of Jesus Christ to raise them out of these destructive patterns and cycles.

Lord, nothing is too hard for You. I pray for those that have been tormented and traumatized by controlling and manipulative parents and/or guardians. Father, allow them to break these demonic strongholds off of their lives, so they can finally live in freedom in You. Reveal Yourself unto them Lord as Father and show them the true, authentic love they so desperately needed from their earthly caregivers. I break off the demonic spirit of narcissism in the lives of these precious people and release newness of life into their weary souls. Bring deliverance Father and set Your people free!

Meet the Author

Dawn D. Christensen was born in St. Louis, Missouri and raised in Washington State. She is a Registered Nurse since 2008, graduating from Renton Technical College. Since then, she has worked in a variety of locations ranging from Operating Room, Pediatrics/Family Medicine, Psychiatric, and Hospice.

Dawn loves sharing the Bemer treatments, prayer, and healing declarations to bring comfort to the bodies and hearts of many, and the love of Christ and His presence. She loves to teach others how pray and declare life over their bodies and/or situations believing for the miraculous and bringing Hope.

Dawn has taken classes on Discipleship, Mentoring, and Supernatural through *Compassion to Action*, *Healing the Northwest Ministries*, and *Care Net Pregnancy & Family Services* where she shares the Gospel and love of Christ, mentors young mothers, and performs ultrasounds.

Dawn is the mother of three, including her son Nathaniel and daughters, Heaven and Nevaeh. She loves spending time with her children, playing the Ukulele and the Guitar, worshiping, evangelism, and teaching and sharing resources with others on how to heal their bodies, both naturally and spiritually.

Bibliography

[i] Lange, J. P., & Schaff, P. (2008). A commentary on the Holy Scriptures: John (p. 356). Bellingham, WA: Logos Bible Software.

[ii] Sexual abuse hotline and other resources.

[iii] *Understanding the Generational Curse of Exodus.* Focus on the Family. https://www.focusonthefamily.com/family-qa/understanding-the-generational-curse-of-exodus-347/.

[iv] *5 Verses on Hope Found in Jesus Christ.* Billy Graham. 23 March 2016. https://billygrahamlibrary.org/5-verses-on-hope-found-in-jesus-christ/.

[v] 39 Different Types of Counselors and Salaries – Guide to Counseling Careers. *Psychology School Guide.* https://www.psychologyschoolguide.net/counseling-careers/.